HOMES WITH A VIEW

175 HOME PLANS FOR GOLF-COURSE, WATERFRONT AND MOUNTAIN HOMES

HOMES WITH A
VIEW

Published by Home Planners, LLC
Wholly owned by Hanley-Wood, LLC

President, Jayne Fenton
Chief Financial Officer, Joe Carroll
Vice President, Publishing, Jennifer Pearce
Vice President, General Manager, Marc Wheeler
Executive Editor, Linda Bellamy
National Sales Manager, Book Division, Julie Marshall
Managing Editor, Jason D. Vaughan
Special Projects Editor, Kristin Schneidler
Editor, Nate Ewell
Associate Editor, Kathryn R. Sears
Lead Plans Associate, Morenci C. Clark
Plans Associates, Jill M. Hall, Elizabeth Landry, Nick Nieskes
Proofreaders/Copywriters, Douglas Jenness, Sarah Lyons
Technical Specialist, Jay C. Walsh
Lead Data Coordinator, Fran Altemose
Data Coordinators, Misty Boler, Melissa Siewert
Production Director, Sara Lisa
Production Manager, Brenda McClary

Big Designs, Inc.
President, Creative Director, Anthony D'Elia
Vice President, Business Manager, Megan D'Elia
Vice President, Design Director, Chris Bonavita
Editorial Director, John Roach
Assistant Editor, Tricia Starkey
Director of Design and Production, Stephen Reinfurt
Group Art Director, Kevin Limongelli
Photo Editor, Christine DiVuolo
Managing Art Director, Jessica Hagenbuch
Graphic Designer, Mary Ellen Mulshine
Graphic Designer, Lindsey O'Neill-Myers
Graphic Designer, Jacque Young
Assistant Photo Editor, Brian Wilson
Project Director, David Barbella
Assistant Production Manager, Rich Fuentes

Photo Credits
Front Cover and Title Page: Photo by Jason McConathy
Facing Page Top: Photo by Raef Grohne Photography
Facing Page Center: Photo by Bob Greenspan
Facing Page Bottom: Photo courtesy of William E. Poole Designs, Inc.; Islands of Beaufort, Beaufort, S.C.
Back Cover: Photo courtesy of Living Concepts.

Hanley Wood HomePlanners Corporate Headquarters
3275 W. Ina Road, Suite 220
Tucson, Arizona 85741

Distribution Center
29333 Lorie Lane
Wixom, Michigan 48393

© 2004

10 9 8 7 6 5 4 3 2 1

Printed in the United States of America

Library of Congress Catalog Control Number: 2003113857

ISBN #: 1-931131-25-2

HOMES WITH A
VIEW

11

18

7

Grab Your Binoculars

and enjoy breathtaking views! All of the homes in this inspiring collection feature designs with open floor plans, large windows, and expansive outdoor living spaces. Architecture teams up with nature to offer the best of resort-style living in your own home. In the first section of this book, you'll find 28 of our finest homes presented in full color. The rest of the book is organized by square footage, conveniently allowing you to search for a home that fits your family's needs.

Throughout, you'll find three logos that can help narrow your search, depending on the location of your lot. One, featuring a flagstick and a golf ball that's a short birdie putt away, highlights homes that are particularly suited for golf course living. Expansive windows make you feel like you're right on the fairway, while a porch or deck let you enjoy the fresh air and watch the duffers make their way towards the nearest hole.

Another logo, featuring a snow-topped mountain, highlights homes with rustic exteriors suited for the mountains. Craftsman homes and cottages are among the most popular choices in mountainside areas, since they blend in well with their surroundings. With an array of windows to look out on the hills, these homes give you every opportunity to appreciate the topography around them.

A third logo showcases a sailboat and seagulls, and highlights designs that are created with waterfront living in mind. Here the gentle sounds of waves meeting the shore will draw you to the water during the day and lull you to sleep at night. Porches, patios, and decks create seamless transitions from indoors to out, making it easy to enjoy the water and the spectacular views it provides.

Of course, all of these homes have one thing in common—an appreciation for beautiful, panoramic vistas. Regardless of your location, take a look at all your options. With 175 plans to choose from, you're sure to find a home that suits both your lot and your lifestyle.

This Mediterranean home offers a dreamy living-by-the-water lifestyle, but it's ready to build in any region. A lovely arch-top entry announces an exquisite foyer with a curved staircase. The family room provides a fireplace and opens to the outdoors on both sides of the plan. An L-shaped kitchen serves a cozy morning area as well as a stunning formal dining room, which offers a bay window. Second-floor sleeping quarters include four bedrooms and two bathrooms. The master suite opens to a balcony and offers a bath with a double-bowl vanity.

plan
HPT9800048

STYLE: MEDITERRANEAN
FIRST FLOOR: 1,065 SQ. FT.
SECOND FLOOR: 1,032 SQ. FT.
TOTAL: 2,097 SQ. FT.
BEDROOMS: 4
BATHROOMS: 2½
WIDTH: 38' - 0"
DEPTH: 38' - 0"
FOUNDATION: BASEMENT

SEARCH ONLINE @ EPLANS.COM

SECOND FLOOR

FIRST FLOOR

Perfect Waterfront Plan

REAR EXTERIOR

plan

HPT9800047

STYLE: TRADITIONAL
FIRST FLOOR: 832 SQ. FT.
SECOND FLOOR: 1,331 SQ. FT.
TOTAL: 2,163 SQ. FT.
BEDROOMS: 3
BATHROOMS: 2½
WIDTH: 37' - 6"
DEPTH: 48' - 4"
FOUNDATION: BASEMENT

SEARCH ONLINE @ EPLANS.COM

This home offers two stories, with a twist! The living spaces are on the second floor and include a living/dining room combination with a deck and fireplace. The family room also has a fireplace, plus a built-in entertainment center, and is open to the skylit kitchen. The master bedroom is also on this level and features a private bath. Family bedrooms, a full bath, and a cozy den reside on the first level.

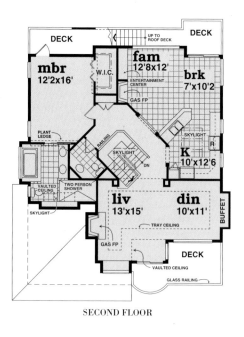

SECOND FLOOR

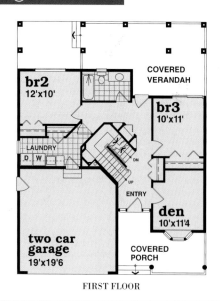

FIRST FLOOR

plan
HPT9800049

STYLE: TRADITIONAL
FIRST FLOOR: 4,208 SQ. FT.
SECOND FLOOR: 1,352 SQ. FT.
TOTAL: 5,560 SQ. FT.
BEDROOMS: 4
BATHROOMS: 4½ + ½
WIDTH: 94' - 0"
DEPTH: 68' - 0"
FOUNDATION: CRAWLSPACE, SLAB

SEARCH ONLINE @ EPLANS.COM

Two-story pilasters create a sense of the Old South on the facade of this modern home, updating the classic Adam style. The foyer opens through an archway, announcing the breathtaking circular staircase. The formal dining room is situated on the right, and the private library is found to the left. The grand family room is crowned with a sloped ceiling. The angled, galley kitchen adjoins the breakfast nook; the butler's pantry facilitates service to the dining room. The master suite finds privacy on the left with an elegant sitting area defined with pillars. Two bedroom suites, each with walk-in closets, share the second floor with the game room.

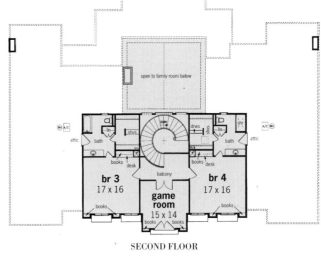

SECOND FLOOR

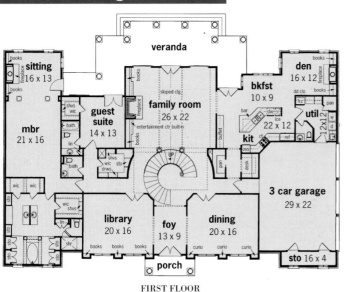

FIRST FLOOR

Wood siding, muntin window dormers, and a double-decker porch exemplify Southern country style in this welcoming plan. Slide off your porch swing and enter through the foyer, flanked by the bayed living room and dining room. The family room flows effortlessly into the breakfast area and the kitchen, complete with an island. The master bedroom wows with a closet designed for a true clotheshorse. Three upstairs bedrooms enjoy access to the upper porch and space for a future recreation room.

plan
HPT9800050

STYLE: FARMHOUSE
FIRST FLOOR: 1,995 SQ. FT.
SECOND FLOOR: 1,062 SQ. FT.
TOTAL: 3,057 SQ. FT.
BONUS SPACE: 459 SQ. FT.
BEDROOMS: 4
BATHROOMS: 3½
WIDTH: 71' - 0"
DEPTH: 57' - 4"
FOUNDATION: BASEMENT

SEARCH ONLINE @ EPLANS.COM

FIRST FLOOR

SECOND FLOOR

plan
HPT9800051

STYLE: COLONIAL
FIRST FLOOR: 2,348 SQ. FT.
SECOND FLOOR: 1,872 SQ. FT.
TOTAL: 4,220 SQ. FT.
BEDROOMS: 4
BATHROOMS: 3½ + ½
WIDTH: 90' - 4"
DEPTH: 44' - 8"
FOUNDATION: BASEMENT

LD

SEARCH ONLINE @ EPLANS.COM

This classic Georgian design contains a variety of features that make it outstanding: a pediment gable with cornice work and dentils, beautifully proportioned columns, and a distinct window treatment. Inside the foyer, a stunning curved staircase introduces you to this Southern-style home. The first floor contains some special appointments: a fireplace in the living room and another fireplace and a wet bar in the gathering room. A study is offered towards the rear of the plan for convenient home office use. A gourmet island kitchen is open to a breakfast room with a pantry. Upstairs, an extension over the garage allows for a huge walk-in closet in the master suite and a full bath in one of the family bedrooms.

QUOTE ONE®
Cost to build? See page 187
to order complete cost estimate
to build this house in your area!

SECOND FLOOR

REAR EXTERIOR

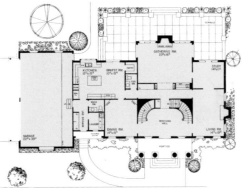

FIRST FLOOR

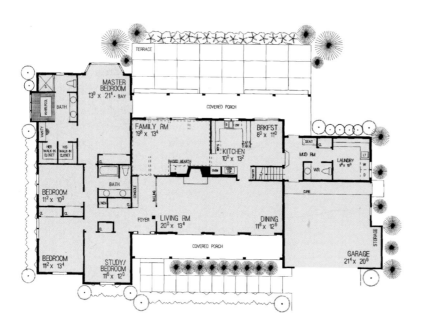

plan (#)

HPT9800052

STYLE: FARMHOUSE

SQUARE FOOTAGE: 2,549

BEDROOMS: 4

BATHROOMS: 2½

WIDTH: 88' - 8"

DEPTH: 53' - 6"

FOUNDATION: BASEMENT   **L**

SEARCH ONLINE @ EPLANS.COM

Covered porches to the front and rear will be the envy of the neighborhood when this house is built. The interior plan meets family needs perfectly in well-zoned areas. The sleeping wing has four bedrooms and two baths. The living area has formal and informal gathering space. A work zone with a U-shaped kitchen shares space with the naturally lit breakfast nook. The laundry and powder room are located in the far right corner of the plan. The two-car garage has a huge storage area.

plan(#)
HPT9800017

STYLE: CRAFTSMAN
MAIN LEVEL: 2,172 SQ. FT.
LOWER LEVEL: 1,813 SQ. FT.
TOTAL: 3,985 SQ. FT.
BEDROOMS: 4
BATHROOMS: 3½
WIDTH: 75' - 0"
DEPTH: 49' - 0"
FOUNDATION: BASEMENT

SEARCH ONLINE @ EPLANS.COM

With the Craftsman stylings of a mountain lodge, this rustic four-bedroom home is full of surprises. The foyer opens to the right to the great room, warmed by a stone hearth. A corner media center is convenient for entertaining. The dining room, with a furniture alcove, opens to the side terrace, inviting meals alfresco. An angled kitchen provides lots of room to move. The master suite is expansive, with French doors, a private bath, and spa tub. On the lower level, two bedrooms share a bath; a third enjoys a private suite. The games room includes a fireplace, media center, wet bar, and wine cellar. Don't miss the storage capacity and work area in the garage.

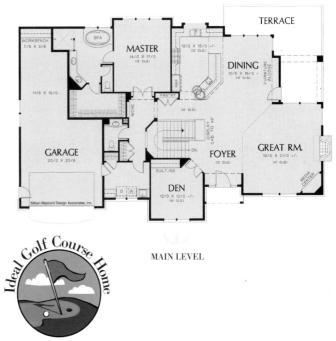

MAIN LEVEL

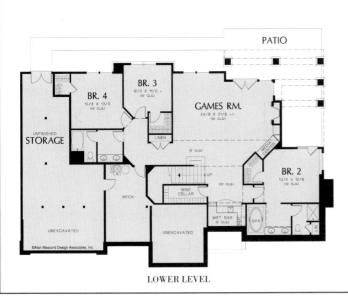

LOWER LEVEL

Craftsman detailing and a hint of French flair make this home a standout in any neighborhood. An impressive foyer opens to the left to the great room, with a coffered ceiling, warming fireplace, and a charming alcove set in a turret. The kitchen is designed for entertaining, with an island that doubles as a snack bar and plenty of room to move. An adjacent porch invites dining alfresco. The bayed study is peaceful and quiet. A nearby guest room enjoys a private bath. Upstairs, the master suite is awe inspiring. A romantic fireplace sets the mood and natural light pours in. A sumptuous spa bath leaves homeowners pampered and relaxed. Two bedroom suites share a vaulted bonus room, perfect as a home gym.

plan ⊕

HPT9800007

STYLE: CRAFTSMAN
FIRST FLOOR: 2,572 SQ. FT.
SECOND FLOOR: 1,578 SQ. FT.
TOTAL: 4,150 SQ. FT.
BONUS SPACE: 315 SQ. FT.
BEDROOMS: 4
BATHROOMS: 4½
WIDTH: 78' - 2"
DEPTH: 68' - 0"
FOUNDATION: CRAWLSPACE

SEARCH ONLINE @ EPLANS.COM

FIRST FLOOR

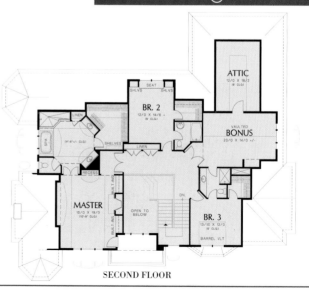

SECOND FLOOR

plan
HPT9800053

STYLE: TRADITIONAL
FIRST FLOOR: 2,514 SQ. FT.
SECOND FLOOR: 975 SQ. FT.
TOTAL: 3,489 SQ. FT.
BEDROOMS: 4
BATHROOMS: 3½
WIDTH: 74' - 8"
DEPTH: 64' - 8"
FOUNDATION: BASEMENT

SEARCH ONLINE @ EPLANS.COM

You are sure to fall in love with what this traditional French Country two-story design has to offer. The great room hosts a fireplace surrounded by built-in cabinets, a two-story ceiling, and striking arched windows. The study will provide you with a corner of the house to yourself with a view out the front and side. The master bedroom enjoys plenty of space and walk-in closets. The master bathroom features a welcoming arch over the bathtub and large shower.

FIRST FLOOR

SECOND FLOOR

The stone-and-brick exterior with multiple gables and a side-entry garage create a design that brags great curb appeal. The gourmet kitchen with an island and snack bar combine with the spacious breakfast room and hearth room to create a warm and friendly atmosphere for family living. The luxurious master bedroom with a sitting area and fireplace is complemented by a deluxe dressing room and walk-in closet. The basement level contains an office, media room, billiards room, exercise area, and plenty of storage.

plan #

HPT9800054

STYLE: TRADITIONAL
SQUARE FOOTAGE: 3,570
BASEMENT: 2,367 SQ. FT.
BEDROOMS: 3
BATHROOMS: 3½
WIDTH: 84' - 6"
DEPTH: 69' - 4"
FOUNDATION: BASEMENT

SEARCH ONLINE @ EPLANS.COM

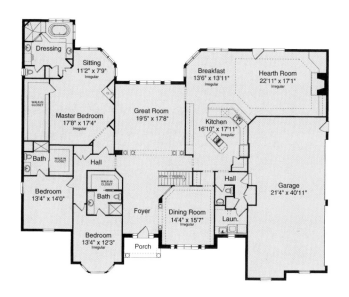

Office 12'10" x 11'8" Irregular

Bedroom 12'6" x 14'11" Irregular

WALK-IN CLOSET

Raised Bar

Billiards Room 19'8" x 15'11" Irregular

Media Area 20'0" x 13'6" Irregular

Hall

Bath

Game Room 14'11" x 9'6"

Unexcavated

Basement

Exercise Area 13'8" x 12'5"

Unexc.

BASEMENT

Dressing

WALK-IN CLOSET

Sitting 11'2" x 7'9" Irregular

Breakfast 13'6" x 13'11" Irregular

Hearth Room 22'11" x 17'1" Irregular

Master Bedroom 17'8" x 17'4" Irregular

Great Room 19'5" x 17'8"

Kitchen 16'10" x 17'11" Irregular

Bath

WALK-IN CLOSET

Hall

Bedroom 13'4" x 14'0"

WALK-IN CLOSET

Bath

Foyer

DOWN 17 RISERS

Dining Room 14'4" x 15'7" Irregular

Hall

Laun.

Garage 21'4" x 40'11"

Bedroom 13'4" x 12'3" Irregular

Porch

plan
HPT9800055

STYLE: TRADITIONAL
FIRST FLOOR: 2,497 SQ. FT.
SECOND FLOOR: 1,167 SQ. FT.
TOTAL: 3,664 SQ. FT.
BEDROOMS: 4
BATHROOMS: 2½
WIDTH: 72' - 4"
DEPTH: 65' - 0"
FOUNDATION: BASEMENT

SEARCH ONLINE @ EPLANS.COM

Lovely peaked rooflines adorn the face of this plan and give prelude to a fine floor plan. A library and formal dining room lie to either side of the entry foyer, which is defined by decorative columns. The great room connects directly to an informal dining space with a pub. The island kitchen is just beyond. The master suite dominates the right side of the first floor and contains a bedroom with a tray ceiling and a bath with a separate tub and shower and two sinks. Three family bedrooms on the second floor revolve around a balcony hall and share a full bath.

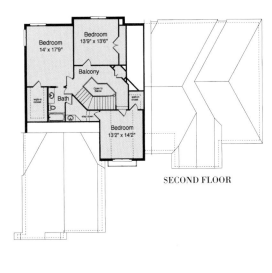

SECOND FLOOR

FIRST FLOOR

A European feel is shown on the facade of this exciting two-story home and hints at the exquisite grace of the interior. The sensational view at the foyer includes high windows across the rear wall, a fireplace, open stairs with rich wood trim, and volume ceilings. The formal dining room offers dimension to the entry and is conveniently located for serving from the kitchen. The spacious breakfast room, wraparound bar in the kitchen, and open hearth room offer a cozy gathering place for family members. The deluxe master suite boasts an 11-foot ceiling, a sitting area, and a garden bath. The second-floor balcony leads to a bedroom suite with a private bath and two additional bedrooms with large closets and private access to a shared bath.

plan #

HPT9800056

STYLE: TRANSITIONAL
FIRST FLOOR: 1,915 SQ. FT.
SECOND FLOOR: 823 SQ. FT.
TOTAL: 2,738 SQ. FT.
BEDROOMS: 4
BATHROOMS: 3½
WIDTH: 63' - 4"
DEPTH: 48' - 0"
FOUNDATION: BASEMENT

SEARCH ONLINE @ EPLANS.COM

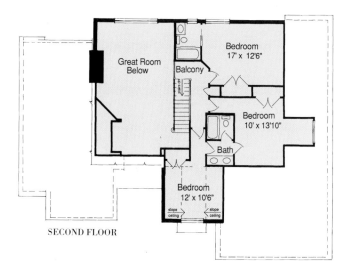

FIRST FLOOR

Dressing
walk-in closet
Master Bedroom 14' x 14'1"
Sitting Area 11'2" x 9'4"
Foyer
Porch
Great Room 16' x 19'6"
Breakfast 14' x 11'2"
Hearth Room 17' x 14'10"
Kitchen
Laun.
Dining Room 12' x 13'10"
Two-car Garage 21' x 20'4"

SECOND FLOOR

Great Room Below
Balcony
Bedroom 17' x 12'6"
Bedroom 10' x 13'10"
Bath
Bedroom 12' x 10'6"
slope ceiling   slope ceiling

plan(#)
HPT9800057

STYLE: TRANSITIONAL
FIRST FLOOR: 2,174 SQ. FT.
SECOND FLOOR: 1,241 SQ. FT.
TOTAL: 3,415 SQ. FT.
BONUS SPACE: 347 SQ. FT.
BEDROOMS: 4
BATHROOMS: 3½
WIDTH: 61' - 4"
DEPTH: 68' - 8"
FOUNDATION: CRAWLSPACE

SEARCH ONLINE @ EPLANS.COM

An impressive facade of stucco, stone, and gabled peaks highlights the exterior of this plan. A loggia welcomes you inside to the foyer flanked by a study/library with a fireplace and the formal dining room brightened by a bay window. A gallery hall leads to other areas of the home, including a guest suite with a private bath, the grand room warmed by an impressive hearth, and the island kitchen overlooking the morning room. Upstairs, the master suite features a private fireplace, His and Hers walk-in closets, and a lavish bath. The second-floor game room is a spacious addition.

FIRST FLOOR

SECOND FLOOR

Now here is a one-of-a-kind house plan. Step down from the raised foyer into the grand gallery where columns define the living room. This central living area boasts an enormous bow window with a fantastic view to the covered patio. The formal dining room is to the right and the lavish master suite sits on the left. The family gourmet will find an expansive kitchen beyond a pair of French doors on the right. The secluded family room completes this first level. An enormous den is found on the first landing above, to the left of the foyer. Two bedroom suites and a loft occupy the second floor.

plan #

HPT9800058

STYLE: TRADITIONAL
FIRST FLOOR: 2,285 SQ. FT.
SECOND FLOOR: 1,395 SQ. FT.
TOTAL: 3,680 SQ. FT.
BONUS SPACE: 300 SQ. FT.
BEDROOMS: 3
BATHROOMS: 3½
WIDTH: 73' - 8"
DEPTH: 76' - 2"
FOUNDATION: SLAB

SEARCH ONLINE @ EPLANS.COM

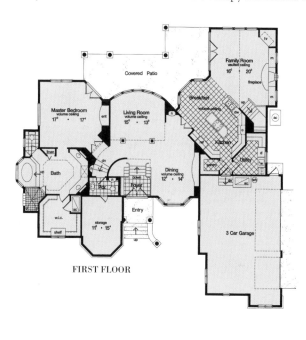

FIRST FLOOR

SECOND FLOOR

plan

HPT9800059

STYLE: TRADITIONAL
FIRST FLOOR: 3,297 SQ. FT.
SECOND FLOOR: 1,453 SQ. FT.
TOTAL: 4,750 SQ. FT.
BEDROOMS: 5
BATHROOMS: 4½
WIDTH: 80' - 10"
DEPTH: 85' - 6"
FOUNDATION: SLAB

SEARCH ONLINE @ EPLANS.COM

This elegant home combines a traditional exterior with a contemporary interior and provides a delightful setting for both entertaining and individual solitude. A living room and bay-windowed dining room provide an open area for formal entertaining, which can spill outside to the entertainment terrace or to the nearby gathering room with its dramatic fireplace. On the opposite side of the house, French doors make it possible for the study/guest room to be closed off from the rest of the first floor. The master suite is also a private retreat, offering a fireplace as well as an abundance of natural light, and a bath designed to pamper. The entire family will enjoy the second-floor media loft from which a balcony overlooks the two-story gathering room below.

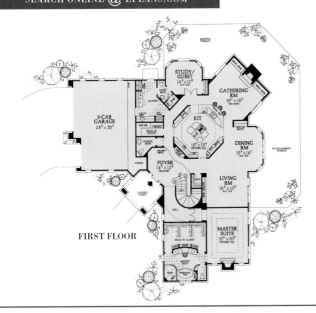

FIRST FLOOR

SECOND FLOOR

Quote One®

Cost to build? See page 187 to order complete cost estimate to build this house in your area!

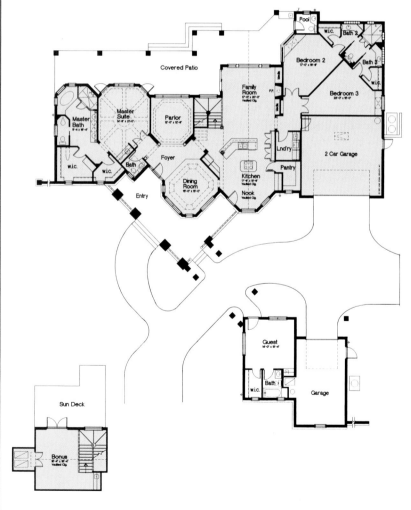

plan #

HPT9800060

STYLE: EUROPEAN COTTAGE
SQUARE FOOTAGE: 3,436
BONUS SPACE: 290 SQ. FT.
BEDROOMS: 3
BATHROOMS: 3½
WIDTH: 94' - 0"
DEPTH: 114' - 0"
FOUNDATION: SLAB

SEARCH ONLINE @ EPLANS.COM

A striking front-facing pediment, bold columns, and varying rooflines set this design apart from the rest. An angled entry leads to the foyer, flanked on one side by the dining room with a tray ceiling and on the other by a lavish master suite. This suite is enhanced with a private bath, two large walk-in closets, a garden tub, a compartmented toilet and bidet, and access to the covered patio. The parlor also enjoys rear-yard views. The vaulted ceilings provide a sense of spaciousness from the breakfast nook and kitchen to the family room. A laundry room and roomy pantry are accessible from the kitchen area. Two family bedrooms reside on the right side of the plan; each has its own full bath and both are built at interesting angles. Upstairs, a vaulted bonus room includes French doors opening to a second-floor sundeck.

plan
HPT9800020

STYLE: European Cottage
FIRST FLOOR: 2,698 SQ. FT.
SECOND FLOOR: 819 SQ. FT.
TOTAL: 3,517 SQ. FT.
BONUS SPACE: 370 SQ. FT.
BEDROOMS: 3
BATHROOMS: 3½
WIDTH: 90' - 6"
DEPTH: 84' - 0"
FOUNDATION: Crawlspace

SEARCH ONLINE @ EPLANS.COM

If you've ever traveled the European countryside, past rolling hills that range in hue from apple-green to deep, rich emerald, you may have come upon a home much like this one. Stone accents combined with stucco, and shutters that frame multipane windows add a touch of charm that introduces the marvelous floor plan found inside. The foyer opens onto a great room that offers a panoramic view of the veranda and beyond. To the left, you'll find a formal dining room; to the right, a quiet den. Just steps away resides the sitting room that introduces the grand master suite. A kitchen with a nook, laundry room, and large shop area complete the first floor. The second floor contains two family bedrooms, two full baths, and a bonus room.

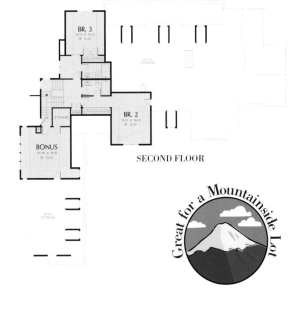

SECOND FLOOR

FIRST FLOOR

Great for a Mountainside Lot

This courtyard design allows for intimate poolside gatherings in complete privacy. Varied ceiling designs create more excitement as you enter through mahogany doors, passing the paved courtyard lavishly appointed with tropical flowers and a pool with a waterfall and spa. The generous master suite features sculptured ceilings; the master bath is sumptuously appointed with grand arches over the spa tub. Two bedrooms upstairs access a private balcony terrace. A privately accessed guest suite/home office rounds out this award-winning design. Note the large summer kitchen near the garage, as well as the intimate sunken powder room tucked under the staircase.

plan #

HPT9800061

STYLE: EUROPEAN COTTAGE
FIRST FLOOR: 2,854 SQ. FT.
SECOND FLOOR: 484 SQ. FT.
TOTAL: 3,338 SQ. FT.
BEDROOMS: 4
BATHROOMS: 3½
WIDTH: 77' - 4"
DEPTH: 94' - 0"
FOUNDATION: SLAB

SEARCH ONLINE @ EPLANS.COM

FIRST FLOOR

SECOND FLOOR

plan
HPT9800062

STYLE: TRADITIONAL
FIRST FLOOR: 3,414 SQ. FT.
SECOND FLOOR: 1,238 SQ. FT.
TOTAL: 4,652 SQ. FT.
BEDROOMS: 4
BATHROOMS: 3½
WIDTH: 90' - 6"
DEPTH: 78' - 9"
FOUNDATION: BASEMENT

SEARCH ONLINE @ EPLANS.COM

Country meets traditional in this splendid design. A covered front porch offers a place to enjoy the sunrise or place a porch swing. With the formal areas flanking the foyer, an open flow is established between the column-accented dining room and the library with its distinguished beam ceiling. The two-story great room features a wall of windows looking out to the rear grounds. On the left, the gourmet kitchen serves up casual and formal meals to the breakfast and hearth rooms with the dining room just steps away. The master bedroom enjoys a sitting area with an array of view-catching windows, a spacious dressing area, and an accommodating walk-in closet. Three family bedrooms—one with a private bath—complete the second level.

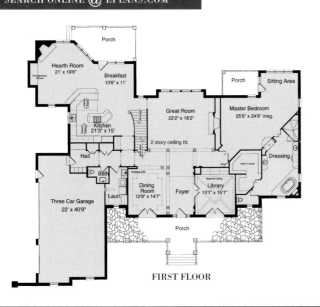

FIRST FLOOR

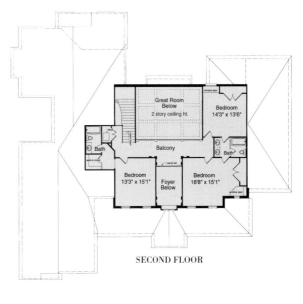

SECOND FLOOR

Climate is a key component of any mountain retreat, and outdoor living is an integral part of its design. This superior cabin features open and covered porches. A mix of matchstick details and rugged stone set off this lodge-house facade, concealing a well-defined interior. Windows line the breakfast bay and brighten the kitchen, which features a center cooktop island. A door leads out to a covered porch with a summer kitchen. The upper level features a secluded master suite with a spacious bath beginning with a double walk-in closet and ending with a garden view of the porch. A two-sided fireplace extends warmth to the whirlpool spa-style tub.

plan
HPT9800063

STYLE: BUNGALOW
FIRST FLOOR: 2,391 SQ. FT.
SECOND FLOOR: 1,539 SQ. FT.
TOTAL: 3,930 SQ. FT.
BONUS SPACE: 429 SQ. FT.
BEDROOMS: 3
BATHROOMS: 3½
WIDTH: 71' - 0"
DEPTH: 69' - 0"
FOUNDATION: BASEMENT

SEARCH ONLINE @ EPLANS.COM

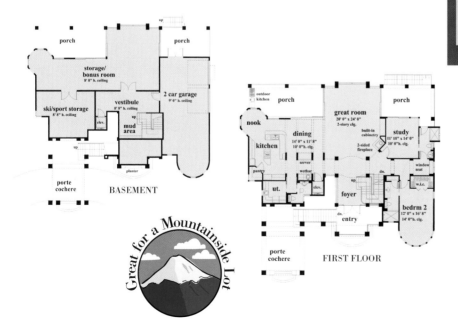

plan
HPT9800064

STYLE: CONTEMPORARY
FIRST FLOOR: 1,414 SQ. FT.
SECOND FLOOR: 620 SQ. FT.
TOTAL: 2,034 SQ. FT.
BEDROOMS: 3
BATHROOMS: 2½
WIDTH: 53' - 0"
DEPTH: 51' - 8"
FOUNDATION: BASEMENT

SEARCH ONLINE @ EPLANS.COM

Attractive, contemporary split-bedroom planning makes the most of this plan. The master suite pampers with a lavish bath and a fireplace. The living areas are open and easily access the rear terrace. Note, in particular, the convenient snack bar between the kitchen and the gathering room/dining room. A large laundry area and washroom separate the main house from the garage. A balcony overlook on the second floor allows views to the gathering room or to the entry.

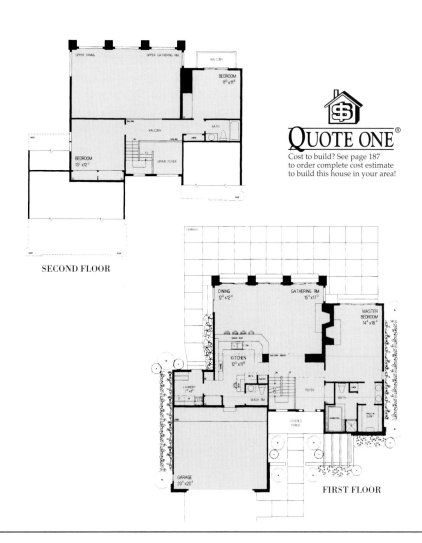

SECOND FLOOR

FIRST FLOOR

QUOTE ONE®
Cost to build? See page 187
to order complete cost estimate
to build this house in your area!

This attractive multilevel home benefits from the comfort and ease of open planning. The foyer leads straight into a large gathering room with a fireplace, and is open to the dining room and kitchen. A perfect arrangement for the more informal demands of today! A media room features a built-in area for your TV, DVD and stereo. The sleeping area features two bedrooms on the upper level—one a master suite with His and Hers walk-in closets. The lower level includes an activities room, a wet bar, and a third bedroom with a full bath.

QUOTE ONE®

Cost to build? See page 187
to order complete cost estimate
to build this house in your area!

plan #

HPT9800065

STYLE: COUNTRY COTTAGE
FIRST FLOOR: 1,327 SQ. FT.
SECOND FLOOR: 887 SQ. FT.
TOTAL: 2,214 SQ. FT.
BASEMENT: 1,197 SQ. FT.
BEDROOMS: 3
BATHROOMS: 2
WIDTH: 39' - 7"
DEPTH: 49' - 4"
FOUNDATION: BASEMENT

SEARCH ONLINE @ EPLANS.COM

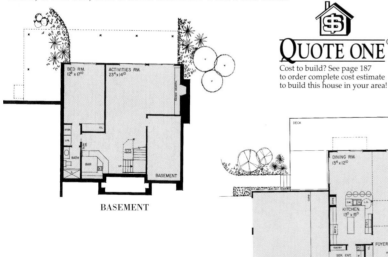

BASEMENT

FIRST FLOOR

SECOND FLOOR

plan

HPT9800066

STYLE: COUNTRY COTTAGE
SQUARE FOOTAGE: 2,151
BONUS SPACE: 814 SQ. FT.
BEDROOMS: 3
BATHROOMS: 2
WIDTH: 61' - 0"
DEPTH: 55' - 8"
FOUNDATION: BASEMENT, CRAWLSPACE

SEARCH ONLINE @ EPLANS.COM

Country flavor is well established on this fine three-bedroom home. The covered front porch welcomes friends and family alike to the foyer, where the formal dining room opens off to the left. The vaulted ceiling in the great room enhances the warmth of the fireplace and wall of windows. An efficient kitchen works well with the bayed breakfast area. The secluded master suite offers a walk-in closet and a lavish bath; on the other side of the home, two family bedrooms share a full bath. Upstairs, an optional fourth bedroom is available for guests or in-laws and provides access to a large recreation room.

SECOND FLOOR

FIRST FLOOR

The unique charm of this farmhouse begins with a flight of steps and a welcoming, covered front porch. Just inside, the foyer leads to the formal dining room on the left—with easy access to the kitchen—and straight ahead to the great room. Here, a warming fireplace and built-in entertainment center are balanced by access to the rear screened porch. The first-floor master suite provides plenty of privacy; upstairs, two family bedrooms share a full bath. The lower level offers space for a fourth bedroom, a recreation room, and a garage.

plan #

HPT9800067

STYLE: FARMHOUSE
FIRST FLOOR: 1,376 SQ. FT.
SECOND FLOOR: 695 SQ. FT.
TOTAL: 2,071 SQ. FT.
BONUS SPACE: 723 SQ. FT.
BEDROOMS: 3
BATHROOMS: 2½
WIDTH: 47' - 0"
DEPTH: 49' - 8"
FOUNDATION: BASEMENT

SEARCH ONLINE @ EPLANS.COM

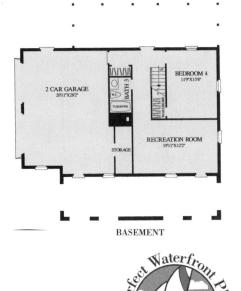

BASEMENT

Perfect Waterfront Plan

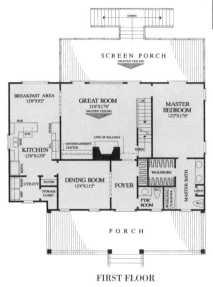

FIRST FLOOR

SECOND FLOOR

plan(#)
HPT9800028

STYLE: FARMHOUSE
FIRST FLOOR: 1,618 SQ. FT.
SECOND FLOOR: 570 SQ. FT.
TOTAL: 2,188 SQ. FT.
BONUS SPACE: 495 SQ. FT.
BEDROOMS: 3
BATHROOMS: 2½
WIDTH: 87' - 0"
DEPTH: 57' - 0"

SEARCH ONLINE @ EPLANS.COM

The foyer and great room in this magnificent farmhouse have Palladian window clerestories to allow natural light to enter, illuminating the whole house. The spacious great room boasts a fireplace, cabinets, and bookshelves. The second-floor balcony overlooks the great room. The kitchen with a cooking island is conveniently located between the dining room and the breakfast room with an open view of the great room. A generous master bedroom has plenty of closet space as well as an expansive master bath. A bonus room over the garage allows for expansion.

SECOND FLOOR

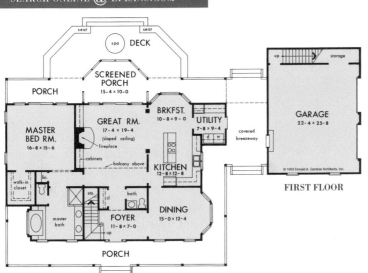

FIRST FLOOR

BONUS RM.
15-4 × 29-4

QUOTE ONE®

Cost to build? See page 187 to order complete cost estimate to build this house in your area!

plan #

HPT9800068

STYLE: FARMHOUSE
SQUARE FOOTAGE: 2,090
BEDROOMS: 3
BATHROOMS: 2½
WIDTH: 84' - 6"
DEPTH: 64' - 0"
FOUNDATION: CRAWLSPACE

L D

SEARCH ONLINE @ EPLANS.COM

This classic farmhouse enjoys a wraparound porch that's perfect for enjoyment of the outdoors. To the rear of the plan, a sun terrace with a spa opens from the master suite and the morning room. A grand great room offers a sloped ceiling and a corner fireplace with a raised hearth. The formal dining room is defined by a low wall and graceful archways set off by decorative columns. The tiled kitchen has a centered island counter with a snack bar and adjoins a laundry area. Two family bedrooms reside to the side of the plan, and each enjoys private access to the covered porch. A secluded master suite nestles in its own wing and features a sitting area with access to the rear terrace and spa.

plan #

HPT9800003

STYLE: COUNTRY COTTAGE
FIRST FLOOR: 1,743 SQ. FT.
SECOND FLOOR: 555 SQ. FT.
TOTAL: 2,298 SQ. FT.
BONUS SPACE: 350 SQ. FT.
BEDROOMS: 4
BATHROOMS: 3
WIDTH: 77' - 11"
DEPTH: 53' - 2"

SEARCH ONLINE @ EPLANS.COM

A lovely arch-top window and a wraparound porch set off this country exterior. Inside, formal rooms open off the foyer, which leads to a spacious great room. This living area provides a fireplace and access to a screened porch with a cathedral ceiling. Bay windows allow natural light into the breakfast area and formal dining room. The master suite features a spacious bath and access to a private area of the rear porch. Two second-floor bedrooms share a bath and a balcony hall that offers an overlook to the great room.

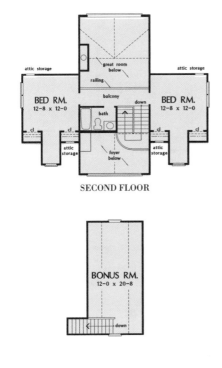

SECOND FLOOR

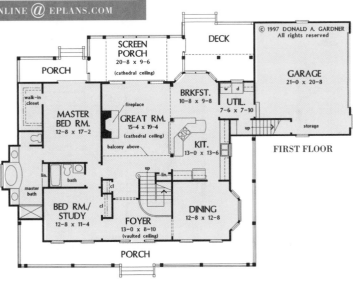

FIRST FLOOR

BONUS RM.
12-0 x 20-8

Perfect for waterfront property, this home boasts windows everywhere. Inside, open planning can be found in the living room, which offers a corner fireplace for cool evenings and blends beautifully into the dining and kitchen areas. All areas enjoy windowed views. A laundry room is conveniently nestled between the kitchen and the two-car garage. The master suite features a walk-through closet and sumptuous bath. Upstairs, three uniquely shaped bedrooms share a full bath.

plan #

HPT9800069

STYLE: CONTEMPORARY
FIRST FLOOR: 1,324 SQ. FT.
SECOND FLOOR: 688 SQ. FT.
TOTAL: 2,012 SQ. FT.
BEDROOMS: 4
BATHROOMS: 2
WIDTH: 55' - 0"
DEPTH: 41' - 0"
FOUNDATION: BASEMENT

SEARCH ONLINE @ EPLANS.COM

FIRST FLOOR

SECOND FLOOR

B·NATHAN·

© 1992 Donald A. Gardner Architects, Inc.

plan #

HPT9800070

STYLE: CONTEMPORARY
SQUARE FOOTAGE: 2,112
BEDROOMS: 3
BATHROOMS: 2
WIDTH: 65' - 0"
DEPTH: 76' - 1"

SEARCH ONLINE @ EPLANS.COM

Indoor/outdoor relationships are given close attention in this plan. Windows on all sides, including dormers in the front and transoms in the great room, let in the view, while sliding glass doors in the sunroom and great room provide access to a spacious deck. Box-bay windows enliven the master bedroom and breakfast area. Other highlights include columns setting off the dining room, and a fireplace and cathedral ceiling in the great room. Two family bedrooms share a full bath. The master bedroom, located on the left side of the plan for privacy, boasts a walk-in closet, twin-basin vanity, garden tub, and separate shower.

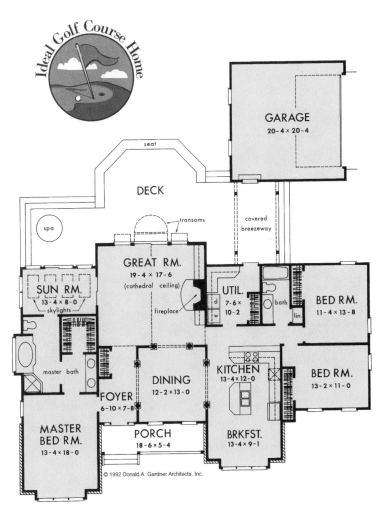

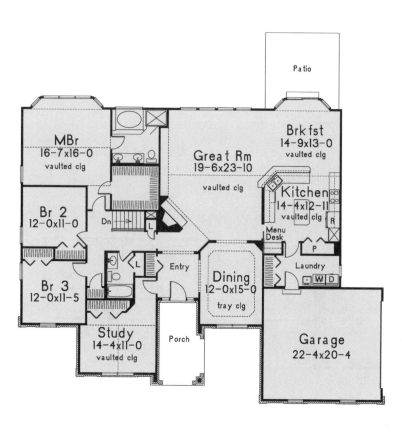

plan#

HPT9800071

STYLE: TRADITIONAL
SQUARE FOOTAGE: 2,483
BEDROOMS: 4
BATHROOMS: 2
WIDTH: 69' - 0"
DEPTH: 53' - 8"
FOUNDATION: BASEMENT

SEARCH ONLINE @ EPLANS.COM

This elegant traditional home is distinguished by its brick exterior and arched entryway with keystone accent. The entryway opens on the right to a formal dining room with an attractive tray ceiling. On the left, a private study—or make it a fourth bedroom—boasts a vaulted ceiling and a picture window with sunburst transom. Family living space includes a vaulted great room with a corner fireplace and a gourmet kitchen with an adjacent breakfast room. Special features in the kitchen include a breakfast bar, center island, menu desk, and pantry. The fabulous master suite enjoys a bay window, large bath, walk-in closet, and vaulted ceiling. Two family bedrooms sharing a full hall bath complete the plan. An unfinished basement provides room for future expansion.

plan#

HPT9800072

STYLE: TRADITIONAL
SQUARE FOOTAGE: 2,349
BONUS SPACE: 850 SQ. FT.
BEDROOMS: 3
BATHROOMS: 2½
WIDTH: 79' - 4"
DEPTH: 59' - 6"
FOUNDATION: BASEMENT

SEARCH ONLINE @ EPLANS.COM

Sunbursts over the entryway and front windows add sophistication to this home. The mix of stone and siding adds a versatile feel to this pleasant home. The rear of this home offers plenty of natural lighting as well as porch space. The grand-scale kitchen features bay-shaped cabinetry overlooking an atrium with a two-story window wall. A second atrium dominates the master suite, which boasts a bayed sitting area and a luxurious bath with a whirlpool tub. The lower level contains a study, family room, and unfinished space for future expansion.

REAR EXTERIOR

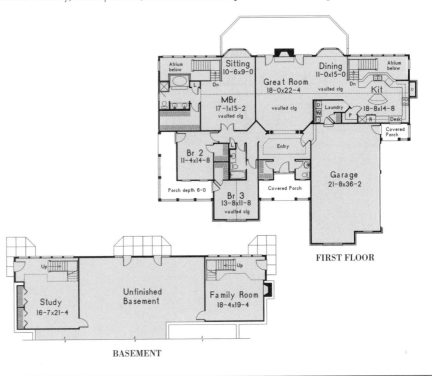

FIRST FLOOR

BASEMENT

Quote One®

Cost to build? See page 187 to order complete cost estimate to build this house in your area!

plan #

HPT9800073

STYLE: FARMHOUSE

SQUARE FOOTAGE: 2,424

BEDROOMS: 3

BATHROOMS: 2½

WIDTH: 68' - 0"

DEPTH: 64' - 0"

FOUNDATION: BASEMENT

L

SEARCH ONLINE @ EPLANS.COM

This unique one-story plan seems tailor-made for a small family or for empty-nesters. Formal areas are situated well for entertaining—living room to the right and formal dining room to the left. A large family room to the rear accesses a rear wood deck and is warmed in the cold months by a welcome hearth. The U-shaped kitchen features an attached morning room for casual meals near the laundry and a washroom. The master suite sits to the right of the plan and has a walk-in closet and a fine bath. A nearby den opens to a private porch. Two family bedrooms on the other side of the home share a full bath.

plan #

HPT9800074

STYLE: PLANTATION

SQUARE FOOTAGE: 2,497

BONUS SPACE: 966 SQ. FT.

BEDROOMS: 3

BATHROOMS: 3½

WIDTH: 87' - 0"

DEPTH: 57' - 3"

FOUNDATION: BASEMENT,
CRAWLSPACE, SLAB

SEARCH ONLINE @ EPLANS.COM

This symmetrical, elegant home features a gabled porch complemented by columns. The breakfast room, adjacent to the kitchen, opens to a rear porch. The spacious great room provides a fireplace and a view of the patio. A lovely bayed window brightens the master suite, which includes a walk-in closet and a bath with a garden tub and a separate shower. Two secondary bedrooms each offer a private bath. A winding staircase leads to second-level future space.

A wraparound porch and a second-floor deck add to the warmth and livability of this splendid two-story Victorian home. A large angled kitchen with an adjoining dining area are the hub around which all activity will revolve. A delightful fireplace adds warmth to the living room where French doors lead to the front porch. A utility room and half-bath are tucked away behind the staircase. The family room resides on the second-floor landing and shares the deck with the master suite. Two additional bedrooms and a full bath complete the second floor.

plan #

HPT9800024

STYLE: COUNTRY
FIRST FLOOR: 1,067 SQ. FT.
SECOND FLOOR: 1,233 SQ. FT.
TOTAL: 2,300 SQ. FT.
BEDROOMS: 3
BATHROOMS: 2½
WIDTH: 58' - 0"
DEPTH: 33' - 0"
FOUNDATION: BASEMENT

SEARCH ONLINE @ EPLANS.COM

FIRST FLOOR

SECOND FLOOR

plan # HPT9800075

STYLE: CAPE COD
FIRST FLOOR: 1,387 SQ. FT.
SECOND FLOOR: 929 SQ. FT.
TOTAL: 2,316 SQ. FT.
BEDROOMS: 4
BATHROOMS: 3
WIDTH: 30' - 0"
DEPTH: 51' - 8"
FOUNDATION: CRAWLSPACE

SEARCH ONLINE @ EPLANS.COM

Perfect for a narrow lot, this shingle-and-stone Nantucket Cape home caters to the casual lifestyle. The side entrance gives direct access to the wonderfully open living areas: gathering room with fireplace and an abundance of windows; island kitchen with angled, pass-through snack bar; and dining area with sliding glass doors to a covered eating area. Note also the large deck that further extends the living potential. Also on this floor is the large master suite with a compartmented bath, private dressing room, and walk-in closet. Upstairs, you'll find the three family bedrooms. Of the two bedrooms that share a bath, one features a private balcony.

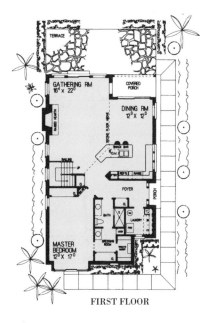

FIRST FLOOR

SECOND FLOOR

REAR EXTERIOR

Cozy and completely functional, this one-and-a-half-story bungalow has many amenities not often found in homes its size. To the left of the foyer is a media room, and to the rear is the gathering room with a fireplace. Attached to the gathering room is a formal dining room with rear-terrace access. The kitchen features a curved casual eating area and island workstation. The right side of the first floor is dominated by the master suite, which offers access to the rear terrace and a luxurious bath. Upstairs are two family bedrooms connected by a loft area overlooking the gathering room and foyer.

plan #

HPT9800076

STYLE: BUNGALOW
FIRST FLOOR: 1,636 SQ. FT.
SECOND FLOOR: 572 SQ. FT.
TOTAL: 2,208 SQ. FT.
BEDROOMS: 3
BATHROOMS: 2½
WIDTH: 52' - 0"
DEPTH: 46' - 2"
FOUNDATION: BASEMENT

LD

SEARCH ONLINE @ EPLANS.COM

QUOTE ONE®

Cost to build? See page 187
to order complete cost estimate
to build this house in your area!

FIRST FLOOR

SECOND FLOOR

REAR EXTERIOR

plan #

HPT9800077

STYLE: NW CONTEMPORARY
SQUARE FOOTAGE: 2,274
BEDROOMS: 3
BATHROOMS: 2
WIDTH: 58' - 0"
DEPTH: 54' - 0"
FOUNDATION: BASEMENT

LD

SEARCH ONLINE @ EPLANS.COM

This attractive bungalow design separates the deluxe master suite from family bedrooms and puts casual living to the back in a family room. The formal living and dining areas are centrally located and have access to a rear terrace, as does the master suite. The kitchen sits between formal and informal living areas, sharing a snack bar with both. The two family bedrooms are found to the front of the plan, with a full bath nearby. A home office or study opens off the front foyer and the master suite.

Quote One®
Cost to build? See page 187
to order complete cost estimate
to build this house in your area!

This Southern Colonial design boasts decorative two-story columns and large windows that enhance the front porch and balcony. Enter through the foyer—notice that the formal dining room on the left connects to the island kitchen. The kitchen opens to a breakfast room, which accesses a side porch that's perfect for outdoor grilling. The great room features a warming fireplace and accesses a rear porch. The master bedroom also includes a fireplace, as well as a private bath with a whirlpool tub and a walk-in closet. A home office, laundry room, and carport complete the first floor. Upstairs, two additional bedrooms share a full hall bath.

plan #

HPT9800078

STYLE: SOUTHERN COLONIAL
FIRST FLOOR: 1,907 SQ. FT.
SECOND FLOOR: 551 SQ. FT.
TOTAL: 2,458 SQ. FT.
BEDROOMS: 3
BATHROOMS: 2½
WIDTH: 58' - 10"
DEPTH: 83' - 7"
FOUNDATION: CRAWLSPACE, SLAB

SEARCH ONLINE @ EPLANS.COM

Carport
23-0x22-0

Office
12-6x13-0

Stor.

Porch
22-5x11-0

Laun.
5-7x8-4

½ Bath

Greatroom
19-2x15-6

Master Bedroom
15-5x15-3

Porch

Breakfast
13-5x9-9

Kitchen
13-5x13-6

Dining
11-11x14-0

Foyer

M.Bath
15-6x13-11

Porch
20-9x9-0

FIRST FLOOR

Bedroom
13-6x11-6

Bath

Bedroom
12-0x14-0

Open to Below

Balcony
20-9x9-0

SECOND FLOOR

REAR EXTERIOR

plan

HPT9800023

STYLE: GEORGIAN
FIRST FLOOR: 1,327 SQ. FT.
SECOND FLOOR: 1,099 SQ. FT.
TOTAL: 2,426 SQ. FT.
BONUS SPACE: 290 SQ. FT.
BEDROOMS: 4
BATHROOMS: 3
WIDTH: 54' - 4"
DEPTH: 42' - 10"
FOUNDATION: BASEMENT, CRAWLSPACE

SEARCH ONLINE @ EPLANS.COM

A Southern classic, this lovely home will become a treasured place to call your own. The entry makes a grand impression; double doors open to the foyer where French doors reveal a study. To the right, the dining room is designed for entertaining with easy access to the angled serving-bar kitchen. A bayed breakfast nook leads into the hearth-warmed family room. Tucked to the rear, a bedroom with a full bath makes an ideal guest room. The master suite is upstairs and enjoys a private vaulted spa bath. Two additional bedrooms reside on this level and join a full bath and an optional bonus room, perfect as a kid's retreat, home gym, or crafts room.

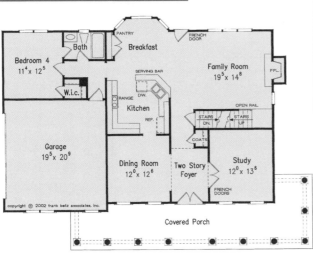

FIRST FLOOR

SECOND FLOOR

A covered front porch, angled walls, dormers and a brick facade create a rich, solid look to this exciting one-and-a-half-story home. Separated by columns and varied ceiling treatments, the great room and formal dining room create a functional gathering area that serves the casual everyday lifestyle equally as well as your special-occasion festivities. An island with seating defines the food preparation area of the kitchen. A delightfully spacious breakfast area with sloped ceiling and multiple windows offers a bright and cheery place to start the day. A covered rear porch offers a relaxed getaway for enjoying the outdoors. A first floor master bedroom suite with a raised ceiling treatment and deluxe bath dazzle the homeowner.

ptan

HPT9800079

STYLE: TRADITIONAL
FIRST FLOOR: 1,925 SQ. FT.
SECOND FLOOR: 524 SQ. FT.
TOTAL: 2,449 SQ. FT.
BEDROOMS: 3
BATHROOMS: 2½
WIDTH: 56' - 4"
DEPTH: 53' - 4"
FOUNDATION: BASEMENT

SEARCH ONLINE @ EPLANS.COM

FIRST FLOOR

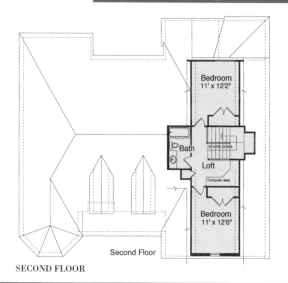

SECOND FLOOR

plan
HPT9800080

STYLE: TRANSITIONAL
SQUARE FOOTAGE: 2,041
BASEMENT: 1,802 SQ. FT.
BEDROOMS: 3
BATHROOMS: 2
WIDTH: 67' - 6"
DEPTH: 63' - 6"
FOUNDATION: BASEMENT

SEARCH ONLINE @ EPLANS.COM

Attention to detail and a touch of luxury create a home that showcases excellent taste, while providing an efficient floor plan. From the raised foyer, a striking view is offered of the great room with its elegantly styled windows and views of the deck. Split bedrooms provide privacy for the master suite, where a sitting area is topped by an exciting ceiling. A garden bath with a walk-in closet and whirlpool tub pampers the homeowner. An optional finished basement adds a recreation room, exercise room, and a guest bedroom.

FIRST FLOOR

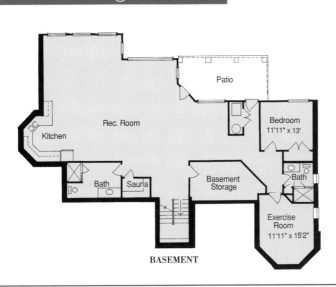

BASEMENT

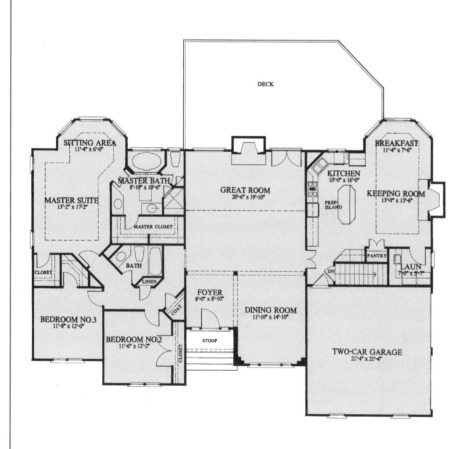

plan #

HPT9800081

STYLE: FRENCH
SQUARE FOOTAGE: 2,295
BEDROOMS: 3
BATHROOMS: 2
WIDTH: 69' - 0"
DEPTH: 49' - 6"
FOUNDATION: WALKOUT BASEMENT

SEARCH ONLINE @ EPLANS.COM

The abundance of details in this plan makes it the finest in one-story living. The great room and formal dining room are loosely defined by a simple column at the entry foyer, allowing for an open, dramatic sense of space. The kitchen with a prep island shares the right side of the plan with a bayed breakfast area and a keeping room with a fireplace. Sleeping accommodations to the left of the plan include a master suite with a sitting area, two closets, and a separate tub and shower. Two family bedrooms share a full bath. Additional living and sleeping space can be developed in the walkout basement.

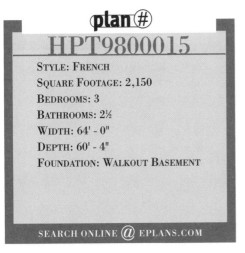

plan (#)

HPT9800015

STYLE: FRENCH
SQUARE FOOTAGE: 2,150
BEDROOMS: 3
BATHROOMS: 2½
WIDTH: 64' - 0"
DEPTH: 60' - 4"
FOUNDATION: WALKOUT BASEMENT

SEARCH ONLINE @ EPLANS.COM

This home draws its inspiration from both French and English Country homes. The great room and dining room combine to form an impressive gathering space, with the dining area subtly defined by columns and a large triple window. The kitchen, with its work island, adjoins the breakfast area and keeping room with a fireplace. The home is completed by a master suite with a bay window and a garden tub.

QUOTE ONE®

Cost to build? See page 187
to order complete cost estimate
to build this house in your area!

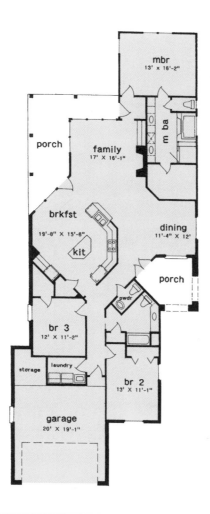

plan #

HPT9800082

STYLE: EUROPEAN COTTAGE
SQUARE FOOTAGE: 2,007
BEDROOMS: 3
BATHROOMS: 2½
WIDTH: 40' - 0"
DEPTH: 94' - 10"
FOUNDATION: SLAB

SEARCH ONLINE @ EPLANS.COM

An ornate stucco facade with brick highlights refines this charming French cottage. The double-door entrance sits to the side—perfect for a courtyard welcome. A dining and family room utilize an open layout for easy traffic flow. The circular kitchen space features an island and complementary breakfast bay. Bedrooms 2 and 3 share a hall bath. The master suite, apart from the main living areas, enjoys privacy and a full bath with a spacious walk-in closet. The rear porch encourages outdoor relaxation.

plan#

HPT9800083

STYLE: MEDITERRANEAN
SQUARE FOOTAGE: 2,367
BEDROOMS: 3
BATHROOMS: 2
WIDTH: 76' - 0"
DEPTH: 71' - 4"
FOUNDATION: SLAB

SEARCH ONLINE @ EPLANS.COM

The impressive entry into this Mediterranean-style home leads directly into a spacious gathering room, with unique angles and a mitered glass window. This is the perfect home for the family that entertains! The large gathering room and covered porch with summer kitchen, are ready for a pool party. Elegance and style grace this split floor plan, with large bedrooms and a very spacious kitchen/breakfast nook area. The kitchen includes a center island and a walk-in pantry. The master suite showcases a fireplace next to French doors, which lead onto the covered porch at the rear, arranged for romantic evenings.

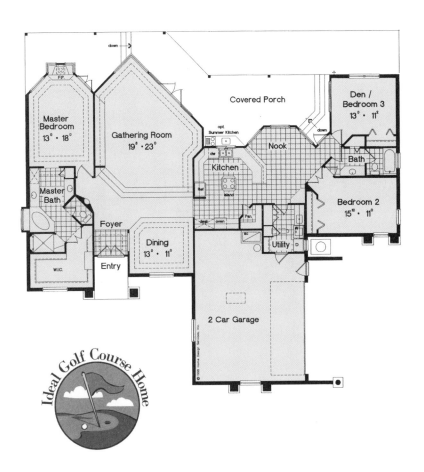

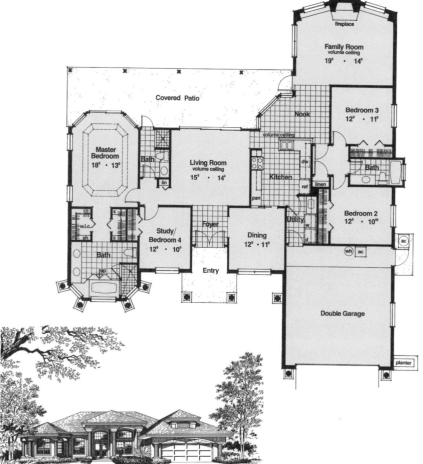

ALTERNATE EXTERIOR

ptan #

HPT9800084

STYLE: CONTEMPORARY
SQUARE FOOTAGE: 2,258
BEDROOMS: 4
BATHROOMS: 3
WIDTH: 66' - 0"
DEPTH: 73' - 4"
FOUNDATION: SLAB

SEARCH ONLINE @ EPLANS.COM

Columns add the finishing touches to this dazzling plan. The double-door entry opens to the foyer, which leads to the vaulted living room with sliding glass doors to the covered patio. The kitchen is open to both the living room and the bayed nook. A bow window and a fireplace define the family room. The master bedroom features access to the covered patio and provides dual walk-in closets and a spa tub. Two additional bedrooms share a full bath.

plan #

HPT9800010

STYLE: CONTEMPORARY

SQUARE FOOTAGE: 2,362

BEDROOMS: 4

BATHROOMS: 3

WIDTH: 65' - 8"

DEPTH: 73' - 4"

FOUNDATION: SLAB

SEARCH ONLINE @ EPLANS.COM

The grand entrance is only the beginning in this well-balanced home. The foyer is centered with the formal living room, with a wall of glass through which to view the outdoor living space. Traffic areas, tiled in marble, add graciousness and practicality as you walk through the home. The master wing has a convenient and versatile den/guest/library adjacent to the master suite entry and poolside bath. The perfectly balanced master bath has a beautiful bay window framing the soaking tub, with matching spaces for the shower and toilet chamber, matching vanities, and walk-in closets.

J.W. HANSEN

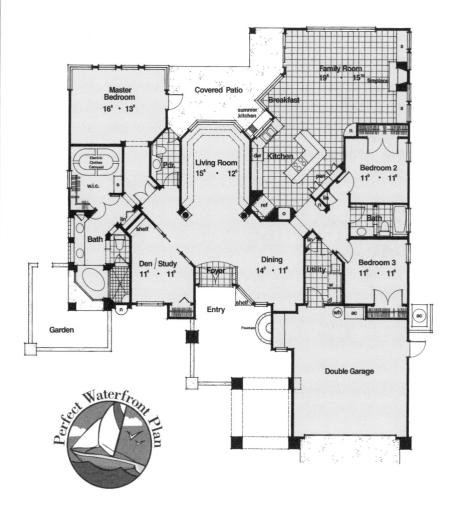

Perfect Waterfront Plan

plan #

HPT9800085

STYLE: CONTEMPORARY
SQUARE FOOTAGE: 2,397
BEDROOMS: 3
BATHROOMS: 2½
WIDTH: 60' - 0"
DEPTH: 71' - 8"
FOUNDATION: SLAB

SEARCH ONLINE @ EPLANS.COM

Low-slung hipped rooflines and an abundance of glass enhance the unique exterior of this sunny one-story home. Inside, the use of soffits and tray ceilings heighten the distinctive style of the floor plan. To the left, double doors lead to the private master bedroom, which is bathed in natural light. Convenient planning of the gourmet kitchen places everything at minimal distances and allows serving the outdoor summer kitchen, breakfast nook, and family room with equal ease.

plan#

HPT9800086

STYLE: CONTEMPORARY
SQUARE FOOTAGE: 2,408
BASEMENT: 1,100 SQ. FT.
BEDROOMS: 4
BATHROOMS: 2
WIDTH: 75' - 8"
DEPTH: 52' - 6"
FOUNDATION: BASEMENT

SEARCH ONLINE @ EPLANS.COM

Contemporary and Mediterranean influences shape the spirit and inner spaces of this new-age home. An arched entrance and front covered porch welcome you inside to the formal dining room and great room. The relaxing kitchen/breakfast area is reserved for more intimate and casual occasions. The master suite provides a walk-in closet and private bath. Bedrooms 2 and 3 share a hall bath. Bedroom 4 makes the perfect guest suite. A family room, sitting area, wet bar, office, and additional bath reside in the baesement.

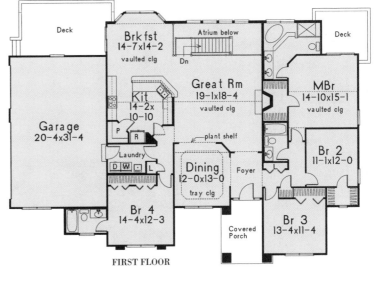

FIRST FLOOR

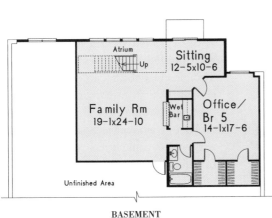

BASEMENT

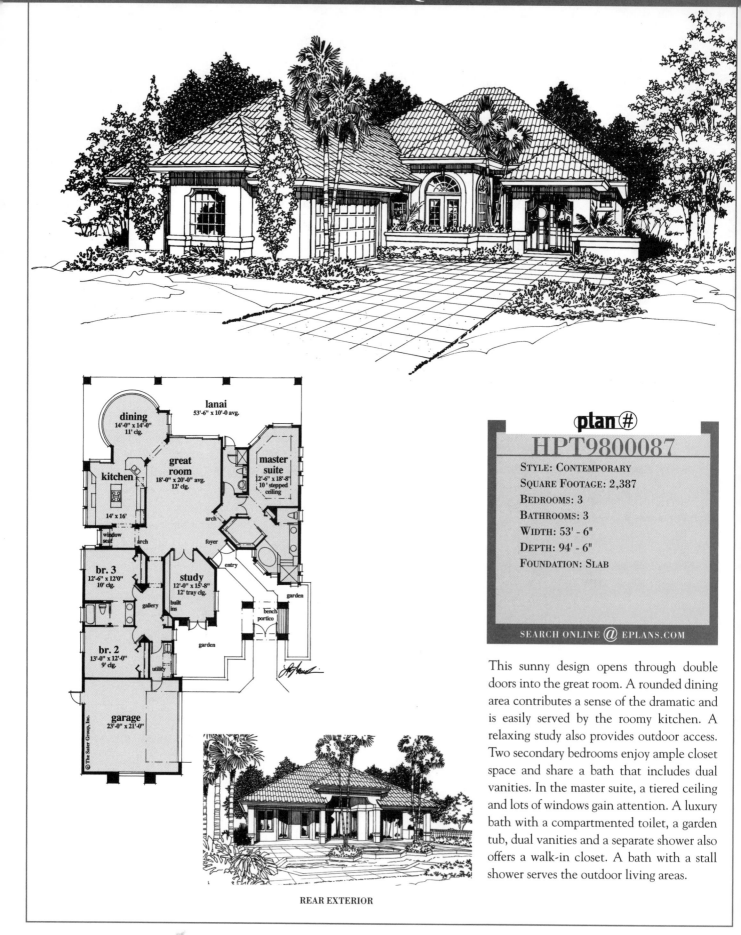

plan #

HPT9800087

STYLE: CONTEMPORARY
SQUARE FOOTAGE: 2,387
BEDROOMS: 3
BATHROOMS: 3
WIDTH: 53' - 6"
DEPTH: 94' - 6"
FOUNDATION: SLAB

SEARCH ONLINE @ EPLANS.COM

This sunny design opens through double doors into the great room. A rounded dining area contributes a sense of the dramatic and is easily served by the roomy kitchen. A relaxing study also provides outdoor access. Two secondary bedrooms enjoy ample closet space and share a bath that includes dual vanities. In the master suite, a tiered ceiling and lots of windows gain attention. A luxury bath with a compartmented toilet, a garden tub, dual vanities and a separate shower also offers a walk-in closet. A bath with a stall shower serves the outdoor living areas.

REAR EXTERIOR

plan
HPT9800088

STYLE: CONTEMPORARY

FIRST FLOOR: 1,522 SQ. FT.

SECOND FLOOR: 800 SQ. FT.

TOTAL: 2,322 SQ. FT.

BEDROOMS: 4

BATHROOMS: 3½

WIDTH: 69' - 6"

DEPTH: 56' - 0"

FOUNDATION: SLAB

L

SEARCH ONLINE @ EPLANS.COM

This two-story Spanish Mission-style home has character inside and out. The first-floor master suite features a fireplace and gracious bath with a walk-in closet, a whirlpool, a shower, dual vanities, and linen storage. A second fireplace serves both the gathering room and media room/library. The kitchen, with an island cooktop, includes a snack bar and an adjoining breakfast nook. Three bedrooms—one a wonderful guest suite—and two full baths occupy the second floor.

FIRST FLOOR

SECOND FLOOR

QUOTE ONE®

Cost to build? See page 187 to order complete cost estimate to build this house in your area!

Multiple rooflines and attractive window treatments introduce this fine three-bedroom home to any neighborhood. Inside, a two-story foyer opens to a sunken living space to the left, which in turn presents a wonderful sunroom. A small, yet cozy office is to the right of the foyer—a perfect location for privacy. The spacious kitchen offers a window sink, built-in planning desk, a serving bar, and easy access to the formal dining room. Note the porch access from both the living and the dining rooms. Upstairs, the lavish master suite shares a deck with one of the family bedrooms and features a private bath, a fireplace, and a huge walk-in closet. The two other family bedrooms share a hall bath.

plan #

HPT9800089

STYLE: CONTEMPORARY
FIRST FLOOR: 1,281 SQ. FT.
SECOND FLOOR: 1,049 SQ. FT.
TOTAL: 2,330 SQ. FT.
BEDROOMS: 3
BATHROOMS: 2½
WIDTH: 68' - 0"
DEPTH: 34' - 0"
FOUNDATION: BASEMENT

SEARCH ONLINE @ EPLANS.COM

FIRST FLOOR

SECOND FLOOR

B. NATHAN

© 1996 Donald A. Gardner Architects, Inc.

plan #

HPT9800090

STYLE: CONTEMPORARY
FIRST FLOOR: 1,750 SQ. FT.
SECOND FLOOR: 604 SQ. FT.
TOTAL: 2,354 SQ. FT.
BEDROOMS: 3
BATHROOMS: 2
WIDTH: 64' - 0"
DEPTH: 42' - 8"

SEARCH ONLINE @ EPLANS.COM

Rustic design invades contemporary detailing. The result? This fine two-story home. The front porch is expected and appreciated as a cozy outdoor retreat. Its mate is found at the back in another porch. The foyer leads to an immense great room with a fireplace and cathedral ceiling, and to its attached formal dining space. This area is open to the U-shaped kitchen and cornered breakfast area. A private bedroom and a bunk room are found to the left of the first floor and share the use of a full bath. You might also turn the bunk room into two separate bedrooms; the choice is yours. The master suite sits on the second level near an attached study loft that overlooks the great room.

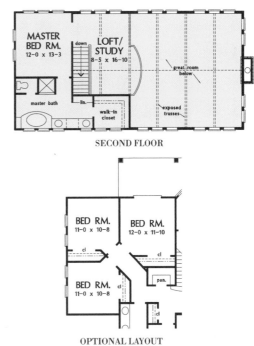

SECOND FLOOR

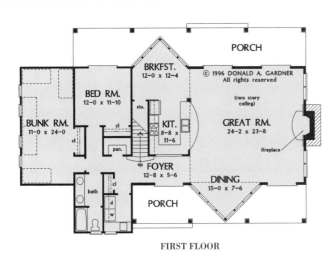

FIRST FLOOR

OPTIONAL LAYOUT

A split staircase adds flair to this European-style coastal home, where a fireplace brings warmth on chilly evenings. The foyer opens to the expansive living/dining area and island kitchen. A multitude of windows fills the interior with sunlight and ocean breezes. The wraparound rear deck finds access near the kitchen. The utility room is conveniently tucked between the kitchen and the two first-floor bedrooms. The second-floor master suite offers a private deck and a luxurious bath with a garden tub, shower, and walk-in closet.

plan #
HPT9800091

STYLE: SEASIDE
FIRST FLOOR: 1,552 SQ. FT.
SECOND FLOOR: 653 SQ. FT.
TOTAL: 2,205 SQ. FT.
BEDROOMS: 3
BATHROOMS: 2
WIDTH: 60' - 0"
DEPTH: 50' - 0"
FOUNDATION: PIER

SEARCH ONLINE @ EPLANS.COM

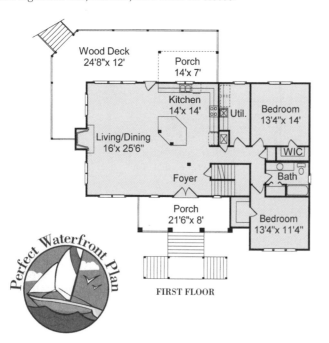

FIRST FLOOR

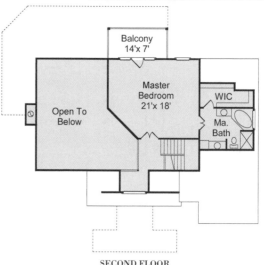

SECOND FLOOR

plan #

HPT9800092

STYLE: TIDEWATER

SQUARE FOOTAGE: 2,190

BEDROOMS: 3

BATHROOMS: 2

WIDTH: 60' - 0"

DEPTH: 54' - 0"

FOUNDATION: BASEMENT

SEARCH ONLINE @ EPLANS.COM

The dramatic arched entry of this cottage borrows freely from the Southern coastal tradition. The foyer and central hall open to the grand room. The kitchen is flanked by the dining room and the morning nook, which opens to the lanai. On the left side of the plan, the master suite also accesses the lanai. Two walk-in closets and a compartmented bath with a separate tub and shower and a double-bowl vanity complete this opulent retreat. The right side of the plan includes two secondary bedrooms and a full bath.

BASEMENT

FIRST FLOOR

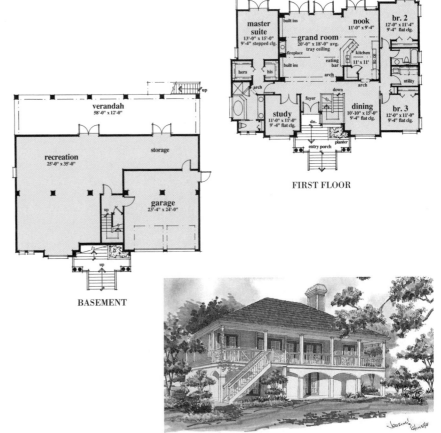

REAR EXTERIOR

Multiple gables, a center dormer with arched clerestory window, and a striking front staircase create visual excitement for this three-bedroom coastal home. Vaulted ceilings in the foyer and great room highlight a dramatic second-floor balcony that connects the two upstairs bedrooms, each with its own bath and private porch. The great room is generously proportioned with built-ins on either side of the fireplace. Private back porches enhance the dining room and the master suite, which boasts His and Hers walk-in closets and a magnificent bath with dual vanities, a garden tub, and separate shower.

plan #

HPT9800093

STYLE: SEASIDE
FIRST FLOOR: 1,620 SQ. FT.
SECOND FLOOR: 770 SQ. FT.
TOTAL: 2,390 SQ. FT.
BEDROOMS: 3
BATHROOMS: 3½
WIDTH: 49' - 0"
DEPTH: 58' - 8"

SEARCH ONLINE @ EPLANS.COM

FIRST FLOOR

SECOND FLOOR

ORDER BLUEPRINTS 24 HOURS, 7 DAYS A WEEK, AT 1-800-521-6797

plan #

HPT9800094

STYLE: CAPE COD
FIRST FLOOR: 962 SQ. FT.
SECOND FLOOR: 1,076 SQ. FT.
THIRD FLOOR: 342 SQ. FT.
TOTAL: 2,380 SQ. FT.
BEDROOMS: 5
BATHROOMS: 3½
WIDTH: 39' - 8"
DEPTH: 36' - 8"
FOUNDATION: PIER

SEARCH ONLINE @ EPLANS.COM

This three-level beach house offers spectacular views all around. With three deck levels accessible from all living areas, the outside sea air will surround you. The first level enjoys a living room, three bedrooms, a full bath, and a laundry area. The second level expands to a family area, a dining room, and a kitchen with an island snack bar and nearby half-bath. The master suite enjoys a walk-through closet and an amenity-filled bath with dual vanities and a separate tub and shower. The third level is a private haven—perfect for another bedroom—complete with a bath, walk-in closet, and sitting area.

THIRD FLOOR

SECOND FLOOR

FIRST FLOOR

Porches and balconies are just the beginning of the amenities provided by this fine two-story home. The foyer opens to the living room, where a fireplace and built-ins warm the ambiance. The open kitchen offers a cooktop island and leads to the dining room. Upstairs, a lavish master suite boasts a private wraparound deck, a walk-in closet, a lavish bath and an adjacent loft—perfect for a computer room or a home office.

ptan#

HPT9800095

STYLE: SEASIDE
FIRST FLOOR: 1,252 SQ. FT.
SECOND FLOOR: 920 SQ. FT.
TOTAL: 2,172 SQ. FT.
BEDROOMS: 3
BATHROOMS: 2
WIDTH: 37' - 0"
DEPTH: 46' - 0"
FOUNDATION: CRAWLSPACE, BLOCK, SLAB

SEARCH ONLINE @ EPLANS.COM

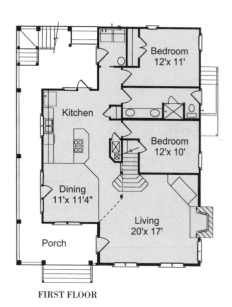

FIRST FLOOR

SECOND FLOOR

© 1999 Donald A. Gardner Architects, Inc.

plan#

HPT9800096

STYLE: SEASIDE
FIRST FLOOR: 1,170 SQ. FT.
SECOND FLOOR: 1,058 SQ. FT.
TOTAL: 2,228 SQ. FT.
BEDROOMS: 4
BATHROOMS: 2½
WIDTH: 30' - 0"
DEPTH: 51' - 0"

SEARCH ONLINE @ EPLANS.COM

A narrow width and front and rear porches make this home perfect for waterfront lots, and its squared-off design makes it easy to afford. The great room, kitchen, and breakfast area are all open for a casual and spacious feeling. Numerous windows enhance the area's volume. Flexible rooms located at the front of the home include a formal living or dining room and a study or bedroom with optional entry to the powder room. Upstairs, every bedroom (plus the master bath) enjoys porch access. The master suite features a tray ceiling, dual closets, and a sizable bath with linen cabinets.

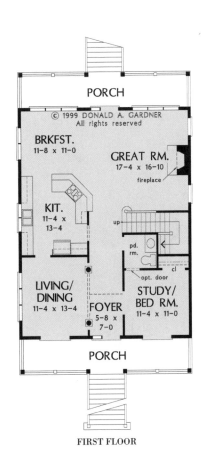

FIRST FLOOR

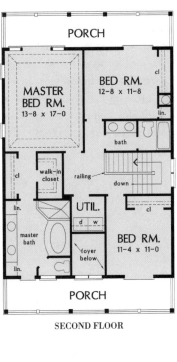

SECOND FLOOR

Perfect Waterfront Plan

With an elevated pier foundation, this stunning home is perfect for waterfront properties. Magnificent porches, a balcony, and a plethora of picture windows take advantage of the beach or lakeside views. The great room features a 10-foot beam ceiling, a fireplace, and a space-saving built-in entertainment center. The staircase is highlighted by a grand window with an arched top, while a Palladian window accents the upstairs loft/study. The master bedroom is the essence of luxury with skylights, a fireplace, cathedral ceiling, balcony, vaulted bath, and oversized walk-in closet. Family bedrooms on the first floor share a full bath. Note the front and rear wrapping porches.

plan #

HPT9800097

STYLE: SEASIDE
FIRST FLOOR: 1,366 SQ. FT.
SECOND FLOOR: 689 SQ. FT.
TOTAL: 2,055 SQ. FT.
BEDROOMS: 3
BATHROOMS: 2
WIDTH: 49' - 4"
DEPTH: 50' - 4"

SEARCH ONLINE @ EPLANS.COM

FIRST FLOOR

PORCH

fireplace

GREAT RM.
14-0 x 16-0

BED RM.
12-0 x 11-0

KIT.
12-0 x 11-0

DINING
12-8 x 11-0

bath

walk-in closet   lin.

FOYER
9-2 x 6-8

UTIL.
6-0 x 8-0

BED RM.
12-0 x 11-0
(cathedral ceiling)

PORCH

(c) 1998 Donald A. Gardner Architects, Inc.

SECOND FLOOR

BALCONY
12-4 x 6-4

MASTER
BED RM.
12-4 x 16-4

skylights

fireplace
(cathedral ceiling)

attic storage

walk-in closet

master bath

handrail

LOFT/
STUDY
10-1 x 11-4
(cathedral ceiling)

down

shelves

palladian window

© 1998 Donald A Gardner, Inc.

plan

HPT9800098

STYLE: SEASIDE

FIRST FLOOR: 1,650 SQ. FT.

SECOND FLOOR: 712 SQ. FT.

TOTAL: 2,362 SQ. FT.

BEDROOMS: 3

BATHROOMS: 2½

WIDTH: 58' - 10"

DEPTH: 47' - 4"

SEARCH ONLINE @ EPLANS.COM

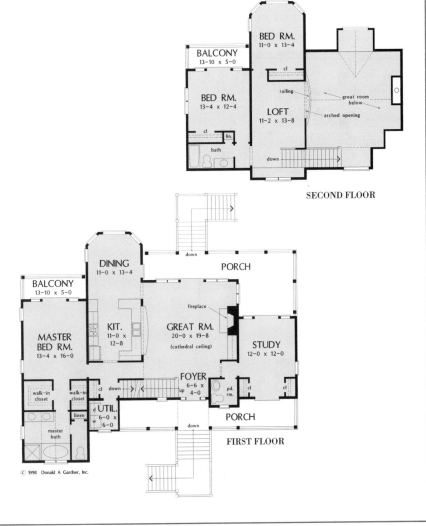

Cedar shakes and striking gables with decorative scalloped insets adorn the exterior of this lovely coastal home. The generous great room is expanded by a rear wall of windows, with additional light from transom windows above the front door and a rear clerestory dormer. The kitchen features a pass-through to the great room. The dining room, great room, and study all access an inviting back porch. The master bedroom is a treat with a private balcony, His and Hers walk-in closets, and an impeccable bath. Upstairs, a room-sized loft with an arched opening overlooks the great room below. Two more bedrooms, one with its own private balcony, share a hall bath.

© 1988 Donald A. Gardner Architects, Inc.

NATHAN INC.

DECK

SUN RM.
11-10×10-0

fireplace

DINING
14-0×12-0

GREAT RM.
14-0×20-0

balcony above

MASTER BED RM.
14-0×14-0

bath

FOYER
6-0×8-0

pd. rm.

walk-in closet

KITCHEN
14-0×13-8

wash dry

storage

down up sta.

UTILITY

down

© 1988 Donald A. Gardner Architects, Inc.

FIRST FLOOR

GARAGE
20-0×19-8

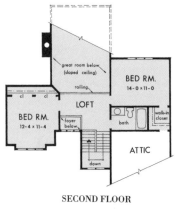

great room below (sloped ceiling)

railing

BED RM.
14-0×11-0

cl cl

LOFT

BED RM.
12-4×11-4

foyer below

bath

walk-in closet

down

ATTIC

SECOND FLOOR

plan #

HPT9800099

STYLE: NW CONTEMPORARY
FIRST FLOOR: 1,479 SQ. FT.
SECOND FLOOR: 576 SQ. FT.
TOTAL: 2,055 SQ. FT.
BEDROOMS: 3
BATHROOMS: 2½
WIDTH: 52' - 8"
DEPTH: 60' - 6"

SEARCH ONLINE @ EPLANS.COM

This striking contemporary home retains a traditional flavor at the front exterior. Inside, the mood is modern and efficient. The formal dining room and the great room open to the sunroom, which has four skylights for passive solar heating. A spacious kitchen allows for a breakfast bar or separate table. The sunroom, great room, and master bedroom offer direct access to the deck, which provides space for a hot tub. The luxurious master bath features a double-bowl vanity, shower, and whirlpool tub. The second level contains two spacious bedrooms sharing a full bath and a loft area overlooking the great room below. Ample attic storage space is provided over the garage.

REAR EXTERIOR

© 1986 Donald A. Gardner Architects, Inc.

plan #

HPT9800100

STYLE: CONTEMPORARY

FIRST FLOOR: 1,434 SQ. FT.

SECOND FLOOR: 604 SQ. FT.

TOTAL: 2,038 SQ. FT.

BEDROOMS: 3

BATHROOMS: 2

WIDTH: 47' - 4"

DEPTH: 69' - 0"

FOUNDATION: CRAWLSPACE

SEARCH ONLINE @ EPLANS.COM

This home's sunroom will delight all with its spiral staircase leading to a balcony and the master suite. The great room enjoys a fireplace and two sets of sliding glass doors leading to the deck. In the kitchen, a U-shape lends itself to outstanding convenience. Three bedrooms include two secondary bedrooms and a glorious master suite. Located on the second floor, the master suite has a fireplace, a generous dressing area with a skylight, and a lavish bath.

FIRST FLOOR

SECOND FLOOR

Great for a Mountainside Lot

This design takes inspiration from the casual fishing cabins of the Pacific Northwest and interprets it for modern livability. It offers three options for a main entrance. One door opens to a mud porch, where a small hall leads to a galley kitchen and the vaulted great room. Two French doors on the side porch open into a dining room with bay-window seating. Another porch entrance opens directly into the great room, which is centered around a massive stone fireplace and accented with a wall of windows. The secluded master bedroom features a bath with a claw-foot tub and twin pedestal sinks, as well as a separate shower and walk-in closet. Two more bedrooms share a bath. An unfinished loft looks over the great room.

plan #

HPT9800101

STYLE: LAKESIDE
SQUARE FOOTAGE: 2,019
LOFT: 384 SQ. FT.
BEDROOMS: 3
BATHROOMS: 2
WIDTH: 56' - 0"
DEPTH: 56' - 3"
FOUNDATION: CRAWLSPACE

SEARCH ONLINE @ EPLANS.COM

REAR EXTERIOR

plan #

HPT9800031

STYLE: FARMHOUSE
FIRST FLOOR: 1,768 SQ. FT.
SECOND FLOOR: 1,120 SQ. FT.
TOTAL: 2,888 SQ. FT.
BEDROOMS: 4
BATHROOMS: 3½
WIDTH: 72' - 0"
DEPTH: 58' - 0"
FOUNDATION: BASEMENT,
CRAWLSPACE, SLAB

SEARCH ONLINE @ EPLANS.COM

A handsome pillared porch welcomes friends and family to this desirable home. The entry is flanked by the formal dining room and a living room that boasts a fireplace and a multitude of windows. A large angled kitchen is nestled between the dining room and the bayed eating area. The master suite enjoys a bayed sitting area and a pampering private bath. Three additional bedrooms and a TV room are found on the second floor. Three porches, a deck, and a courtyard make for wonderful outdoor entertaining possibilities.

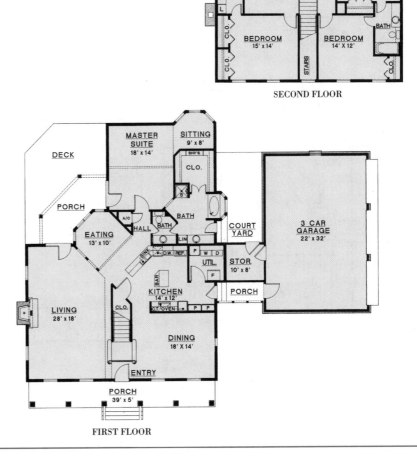

SECOND FLOOR

FIRST FLOOR

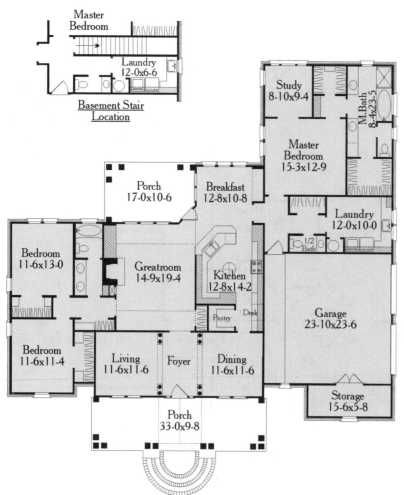

plan #

HPT9800102

STYLE: TRADITIONAL

SQUARE FOOTAGE: 2,570

BEDROOMS: 3

BATHROOMS: 2½

WIDTH: 73' - 0"

DEPTH: 71' - 0"

FOUNDATION: BASEMENT, CRAWLSPACE, SLAB

SEARCH ONLINE @ EPLANS.COM

European charm cleverly frames this home with keystone lintels, columns on the porch, and a sunburst transom over the door. The columned foyer radiates to the living, dining, and great rooms. A fireplace with built-ins sets off the great room. Ribbon windows in the great room, breakfast area, and study take full advantage of the backyard views. The master suite includes a lavish bath, His and Hers walk-in closets, and a private study. The kitchen is full of helpful amenities, such as a built-in desk, large pantry, and snack bar. Two family bedrooms sharing a full compartmented bath finish the plan.

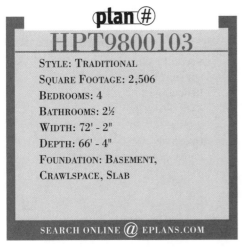

plan #

HPT9800103

STYLE: TRADITIONAL

SQUARE FOOTAGE: 2,506

BEDROOMS: 4

BATHROOMS: 2½

WIDTH: 72' - 2"

DEPTH: 66' - 4"

FOUNDATION: BASEMENT,
CRAWLSPACE, SLAB

SEARCH ONLINE @ EPLANS.COM

A porch full of columns gives a relaxing emphasis to this country home. To the right of the foyer, the dining area resides conveniently near the efficient kitchen. The kitchen island, walk-in pantry, and serving bar add plenty of work space to the food-preparation zone. Natural light fills the breakfast nook through a ribbon of windows. Escape to the relaxing master suite featuring a private sunroom/retreat and a luxurious bath set between His and Hers walk-in closets. The great room features a warming fireplace and built-ins.

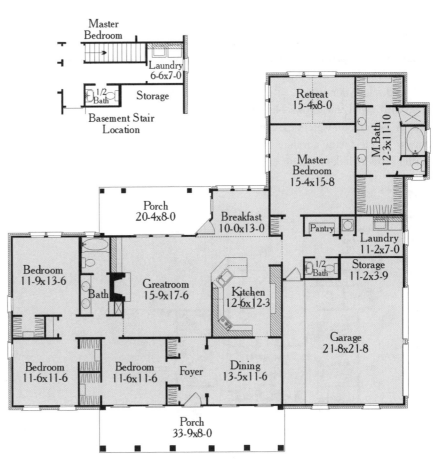

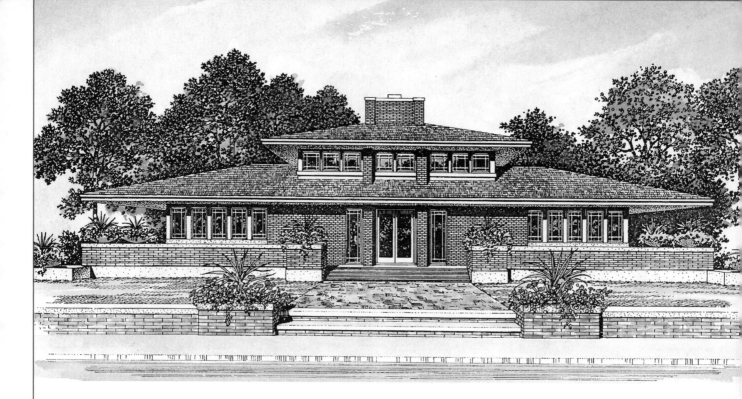

Frank Lloyd Wright had a knack for enhancing the environment with the homes he designed. This adaptation reflects his purest Prairie style complemented by a brick exterior, a multitude of windows, and a low-slung hipped roof. The foyer introduces a gallery wall to display your artwork. To the right, an archway leads to a formal dining room lined with a wall of windows. Nearby, the spacious kitchen features an island snack bar. The two-story family/great room provides an ideal setting for formal or informal gatherings. The left wing contains the sleeping quarters and an office/den. The private master suite includes a sitting area, a walk-in closet, and a lavish master bath.

plan #

HPT9800104

STYLE: PRAIRIE
SQUARE FOOTAGE: 2,626
BEDROOMS: 3
BATHROOMS: 2½
WIDTH: 75' - 10"
DEPTH: 69' - 4"
FOUNDATION: CRAWLSPACE

L

SEARCH ONLINE @ EPLANS.COM

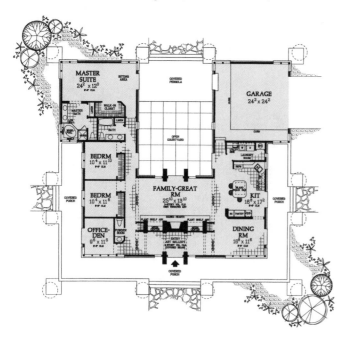

REAR EXTERIOR

Quote One®

Cost to build? See page 187
to order complete cost estimate
to build this house in your area!

plan
HPT9800021

STYLE: BUNGALOW

FIRST FLOOR: 1,798 SQ. FT.

SECOND FLOOR: 900 SQ. FT.

TOTAL: 2,698 SQ. FT.

BEDROOMS: 3

BATHROOMS: 3

WIDTH: 54' - 0"

DEPTH: 57' - 0"

FOUNDATION: CRAWLSPACE

SEARCH ONLINE @ EPLANS.COM

This rustic stone-and-siding exterior with Craftsman influences includes a multitude of windows flooding the interior with natural light. The foyer opens to the great room, which is complete with three sets of French doors and a two-sided fireplace. The master suite offers an expansive private bath, two large walk-in closets, a bay window, and a tray ceiling. The dining room, kitchen, and utility room make an efficient trio.

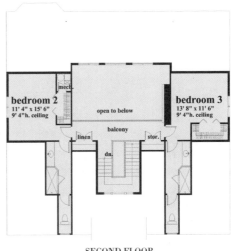

SECOND FLOOR

FIRST FLOOR

A welcoming front porch lined by graceful columns introduces this fine farmhouse. Inside, the foyer leads through an elegant arch to the spacious great room, which features a fireplace and built-ins. The formal dining room and sunny breakfast room flank a highly efficient kitchen—complete with a pantry and a serving bar. Located on the first floor for privacy, the master suite is filled with pampering amenities. Upstairs, two large bedrooms each provide a private bath and walk-in closet.

plan #

HPT9800105

STYLE: COUNTRY COTTAGE
FIRST FLOOR: 1,694 SQ. FT.
SECOND FLOOR: 874 SQ. FT.
TOTAL: 2,568 SQ. FT.
BONUS SPACE: 440 SQ. FT.
BEDROOMS: 3
BATHROOMS: 3½
WIDTH: 74' - 2"
DEPTH: 46' - 8"
FOUNDATION: BASEMENT,
CRAWLSPACE, SLAB

SEARCH ONLINE @ EPLANS.COM

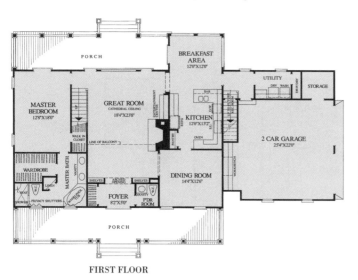

FIRST FLOOR

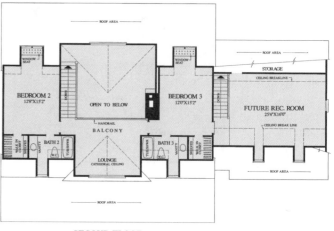

SECOND FLOOR

© 1997 Donald A. Gardner Architects, Inc.

plan#
HPT9800106

STYLE: COUNTRY COTTAGE
FIRST FLOOR: 1,939 SQ. FT.
SECOND FLOOR: 657 SQ. FT.
TOTAL: 2,596 SQ. FT.
BONUS SPACE: 386 SQ. FT.
BEDROOMS: 4
BATHROOMS: 3
WIDTH: 80' - 10"
DEPTH: 55' - 8"

SEARCH ONLINE @ EPLANS.COM

This country farmhouse offers an inviting wraparound porch for comfort and three gabled dormers for style. The foyer leads to a generous great room with an extended-hearth fireplace, vaulted ceiling, and access to the back covered porch. The first-floor master suite enjoys a sunny bay window and features a private bath with a cathedral ceiling, large oval tub set near a window, separate shower, and dual-vanity sinks. Upstairs, two family bedrooms share an elegant bath that has a cathedral ceiling. An optional bonus room over the garage allows plenty of room to grow.

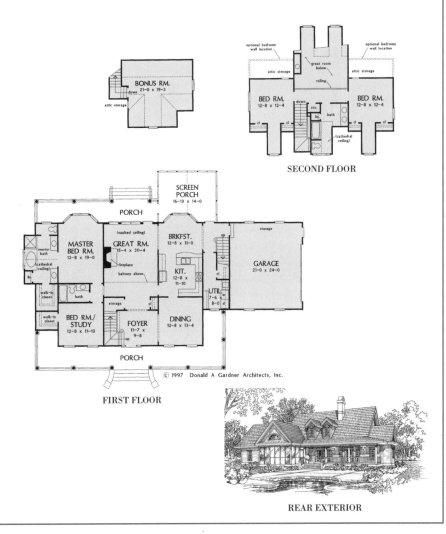

BONUS RM.
21-0 x 19-3

SECOND FLOOR

FIRST FLOOR

© 1997 Donald A Gardner Architects, Inc.

REAR EXTERIOR

This enchanting farmhouse brings the past to life with plenty of modern amenities. An open-flow kitchen/breakfast area and family room combination is the heart of the home, opening up to the screened porch and enjoying the warmth of a fireplace. For more formal occasions, the foyer is flanked by a living room on the left and a dining room on the right. An elegant master bedroom, complete with a super-size walk-in closet, is tucked away quietly behind the garage. Three more bedrooms reside upstairs, along with two full baths and a future recreation room.

plan #

HPT9800107

STYLE: FARMHOUSE
FIRST FLOOR: 1,913 SQ. FT.
SECOND FLOOR: 997 SQ. FT.
TOTAL: 2,910 SQ. FT.
BONUS SPACE: 377 SQ. FT.
BEDROOMS: 4
BATHROOMS: 3½
WIDTH: 63' - 0"
DEPTH: 59' - 4"
FOUNDATION: BASEMENT,
CRAWLSPACE, SLAB

SEARCH ONLINE @ EPLANS.COM

FIRST FLOOR

SECOND FLOOR

plan
HPT9800001

STYLE: VICTORIAN
FIRST FLOOR: 1,734 SQ. FT.
SECOND FLOOR: 1,091 SQ. FT.
TOTAL: 2,825 SQ. FT.
BONUS SPACE: 488 SQ. FT.
BEDROOMS: 4
BATHROOMS: 3½
WIDTH: 57' - 6"
DEPTH: 80' - 11"
FOUNDATION: BASEMENT, CRAWLSPACE

SEARCH ONLINE @ EPLANS.COM

Wonderful Victorian charm combines with the flavor of country in this delightful two-story home. A wraparound porch with a gazebo corner welcomes you into the foyer, where the formal dining room waits to the left and a spacious, two-story great room is just ahead. Here, a fireplace, built-ins, and backyard access add to the charm. The L-shaped kitchen features a work-top island, a walk-in pantry, and a breakfast area. Located on the first floor for privacy, the master suite offers a large walk-in closet and a pampering bath. Upstairs, three bedrooms—one with a private bath—share access to a study loft.

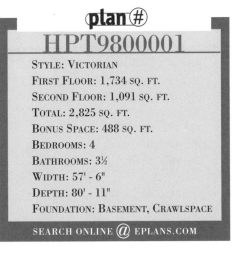

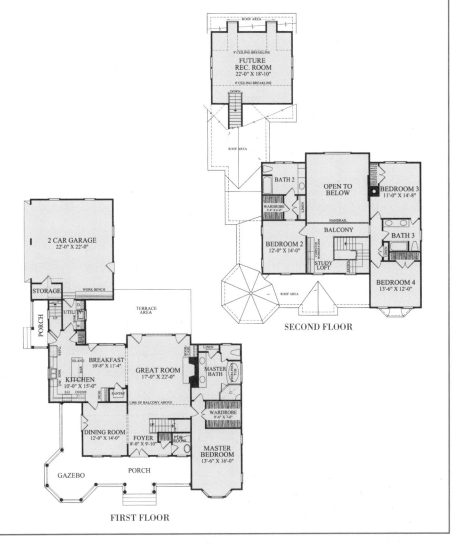

FIRST FLOOR

SECOND FLOOR

SECOND FLOOR

Bedroom 4
13⁹ · 10⁴

Bath.

Loft

Bedroom 3
11⁸ · 10⁴

Bedroom 2
11⁸ · 11⁰

seat

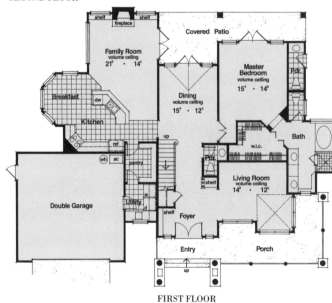

FIRST FLOOR

fireplace

Family Room
volume ceiling
21⁰ · 14⁴

Covered Patio

Breakfast

Kitchen

dw

Dining
volume ceiling
15⁴ · 12⁹

Master
Bedroom
volume ceiling
15⁴ · 14⁰

Pdr.

ref

wh

ac

pantry

up

Bath

w.i.c.

Pdr.

Living Room
volume ceiling
14⁰ · 12⁹

shelf

Double Garage

Utility

shelf

Foyer

Entry

Porch

up

ptan

HPT9800108

STYLE: COUNTRY COTTAGE
SQUARE FOOTAGE: 2,816
BONUS SPACE: 290 SQ. FT.
GUEST SUITE: 714 SQ. FT.
BEDROOMS: 3
BATHROOMS: 3½ + ½
WIDTH: 94' - 0"
DEPTH: 113' - 5"
FOUNDATION: SLAB

SEARCH ONLINE @ EPLANS.COM

Though designed as a grand estate, this home retains the warmth of a country manor with intimate details, on the inside and out. A one-of-a-kind drive court leads to private parking and ends in a two-car garage; a separate guest house is replete with angled walls and sculptured ceilings. A continuous vault follows from the family room through the kitchen and nook. The vault soars even higher in the bonus room with a sundeck upstairs. Two exquisitely appointed family bedrooms with window seats and walk-in closets share a full bath. The master suite has pampering details such as a juice bar and media wall, walk-in closets, and covered patio access.

plan
HPT9800035

STYLE: COUNTRY COTTAGE
FIRST FLOOR: 1,752 SQ. FT.
SECOND FLOOR: 906 SQ. FT.
TOTAL: 2,658 SQ. FT.
BEDROOMS: 4
BATHROOMS: 3½
WIDTH: 74' - 0"
DEPTH: 51' - 7"
FOUNDATION: Basement

L D

SEARCH ONLINE @ EPLANS.COM

Delightfully proportioned and superbly symmetrical, this Victorian farmhouse has lots of curb appeal. The wraparound porch offers rustic columns and railings, and broad steps present easy access to the front, rear, and side yards. Archways, display niches, and columns help define the great room, which offers a fireplace framed by views to the rear property. A formal parlor and a dining room flank the reception hall, and each offers a bay window. The master suite boasts two sets of French doors to the wraparound porch and a private bath with a clawfoot tub, twin lavatories, a walk-in closet, and a stall shower. Upstairs, a spacious office/den adjoins two family bedrooms, each with a private bath.

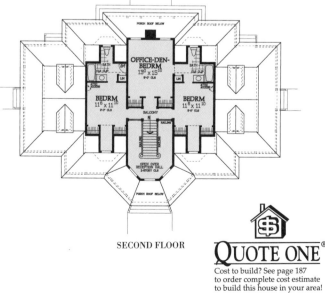

SECOND FLOOR

QUOTE ONE®

Cost to build? See page 187 to order complete cost estimate to build this house in your area!

FIRST FLOOR

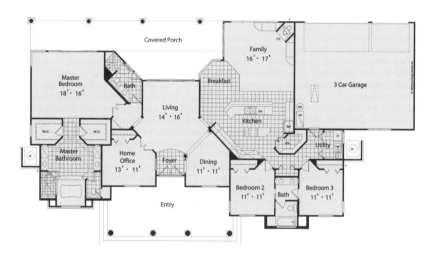

Great for a Mountainside Lot

plan #

HPT9800109

STYLE: FARMHOUSE
SQUARE FOOTAGE: 2,636
BEDROOMS: 4
BATHROOMS: 3
WIDTH: 96' - 6"
DEPTH: 52' - 4"
FOUNDATION: SLAB

SEARCH ONLINE @ EPLANS.COM

This home makes a commanding presence with its country porch and stone-veneer accents. Upon entering, views throughout the home are enjoyed as this plan reaches out in all directions. The living room has a wall of glass to the covered patio, and the dining room, with its decorative columns and angular wall, creates an impressive space. The master suite is welcomed through double doors with a decorative niche nearby. The family living area of this home is just as impressive, with a massive island kitchen serving as the centerpiece. The generous nook can accommodate a large family, as can the family room with its media/fireplace wall.

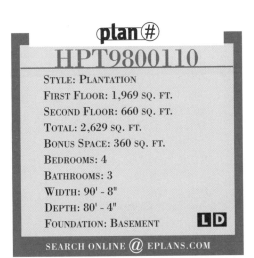

plan #

HPT9800110

STYLE: PLANTATION
FIRST FLOOR: 1,969 SQ. FT.
SECOND FLOOR: 660 SQ. FT.
TOTAL: 2,629 SQ. FT.
BONUS SPACE: 360 SQ. FT.
BEDROOMS: 4
BATHROOMS: 3
WIDTH: 90' - 8"
DEPTH: 80' - 4"
FOUNDATION: BASEMENT

LD

SEARCH ONLINE @ EPLANS.COM

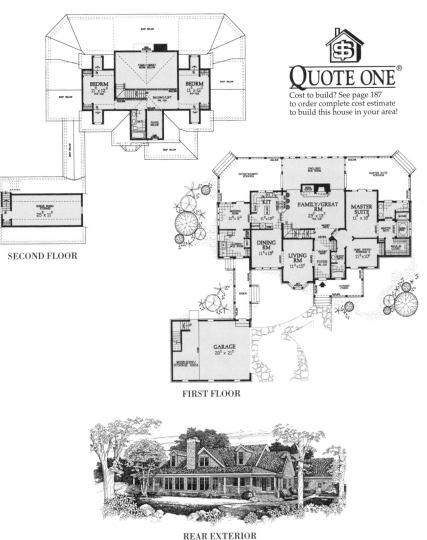

SECOND FLOOR

FIRST FLOOR

Quote One®
Cost to build? See page 187
to order complete cost estimate
to build this house in your area!

REAR EXTERIOR

Varying roof planes, gables, and dormers help create the unique character of this house. Inside, the family/great room gains attention with its high ceiling, fireplace/media-center wall, view of the upstairs balcony, and French doors to the sunroom. In the U-shaped kitchen, an island work surface, a planning desk, and a pantry are added conveniences. The spacious master suite can function with the home office, library, or private sitting room. Its direct access to the huge raised veranda provides an ideal private outdoor haven for relaxation. The second floor contains two bedrooms and a bath. The garage features a workshop area and stairway to a second-floor storage or multipurpose room.

Gables, rafter tails, pillars supporting the shed roof over the porch, and window detailing all bring the flavor of Craftsman styling to your neighborhood with a touch of grace. This spacious home has a place for everyone. The angled kitchen, with a work island, peninsular sink, and plenty of counter and cabinet space will offer the family many a gourmet treat. The spacious gathering room offers a warming fireplace, built-ins, and access to a rear terrace. Upstairs, two suites, each with a private bath, share an open area known as the linkside retreat. Here, access is available to a small veranda, perfect for watching sunsets.

plan#
HPT9800039

STYLE: COUNTRY COTTAGE
FIRST FLOOR: 1,662 SQ. FT.
SECOND FLOOR: 882 SQ. FT.
TOTAL: 2,544 SQ. FT.
BEDROOMS: 3
BATHROOMS: 3½
WIDTH: 59' - 0"
DEPTH: 59' - 6"
FOUNDATION: CRAWLSPACE

SEARCH ONLINE @ EPLANS.COM

FIRST FLOOR

SECOND FLOOR

plan
HPT9800111

STYLE: BUNGALOW
FIRST FLOOR: 2,078 SQ. FT.
SECOND FLOOR: 823 SQ. FT.
TOTAL: 2,901 SQ. FT.
BEDROOMS: 3
BATHROOMS: 2½
WIDTH: 88' - 5"
DEPTH: 58' - 3"
FOUNDATION: BASEMENT

SEARCH ONLINE @ EPLANS.COM

The strong impact of its exterior design will make this home look good in the country or the suburbs. Upon entering, guests are greeted with the expansive great room's cathedral ceiling and cozy fireplace. The kitchen has a snack-counter island with a breakfast nook that opens to a deck. Located on the first floor for privacy, the master suite contains plenty of windows, two walk-in closets, and a whirlpool tub with views out a bayed window. The immaculate second floor overlooks the great room and entryway. A lounge area is flanked by Bedrooms 2 and 3. A full bath with dual vanities completes the plan.

SECOND FLOOR

FIRST FLOOR

Siding and shingles give this home a Craftsman look while columns and gables suggest a more traditional style. The foyer opens to a short flight of stairs that leads to the great room, which features a lovely coffered ceiling, a fireplace, built-ins, and French doors to the rear veranda. To the left, the open, island kitchen enjoys a pass-through to the great room and easy service to the dining bay. The secluded master suite has two walk-in closets, a luxurious bath, and veranda access. Upstairs, two family bedrooms enjoy their own full baths and share a loft area.

plan #

HPT9800016

STYLE: BUNGALOW
FIRST FLOOR: 2,096 SQ. FT.
SECOND FLOOR: 892 SQ. FT.
TOTAL: 2,988 SQ. FT.
BEDROOMS: 3
BATHROOMS: 3½
WIDTH: 56' - 0"
DEPTH: 54' - 0"
FOUNDATION: BASEMENT

SEARCH ONLINE @ EPLANS.COM

BASEMENT

FIRST FLOOR

SECOND FLOOR

plan

HPT9800112

STYLE: COUNTRY COTTAGE
FIRST FLOOR: 1,824 SQ. FT.
SECOND FLOOR: 842 SQ. FT.
TOTAL: 2,666 SQ. FT.
BONUS SPACE: 267 SQ. FT.
BEDROOMS: 3
BATHROOMS: 3½
WIDTH: 59' - 0"
DEPTH: 53' - 6"
FOUNDATION: Crawlspace

SEARCH ONLINE @ EPLANS.COM

Horizontal siding, double-hung windows, and European gables lend a special charm to this contemporary home. The formal dining room opens from the foyer and offers a wet bar and a box-bay window. The great room features a fireplace and opens to a golf porch as well as a charming side porch. A well-lit kitchen contains a cooktop island counter and two pantries. The first-floor master suite has a tray ceiling, a box-bay window, and a deluxe bath with a garden tub and an angled shower. Both of the upper-level bedrooms privately access a full bath.

SECOND FLOOR

FIRST FLOOR

© 1999 Donald A. Gardner, Inc.

UPPER LEVEL

BED RM.
11-8 x 13-0

great room
below

lin.
bath

BED RM.
11-8 x 12-4

railing

foyer
below

down

down

BONUS RM.
12-8 x 41-0

MAIN LEVEL

©1999 Donald A. Gardner, Inc.

PORCH

MASTER
BED RM.
14-0 x 16-0

GREAT RM.
21-0 x 16-0

(cathedral ceiling)

fireplace

balcony above

DINING
12-0 x 15-0

SCREEN
PORCH
9-4 x 9-0

KIT.

BRKFST.
10-0 x 10-0

walk-in
closet

master bath

cl

FOYER
6-4 x
7-4

pd. rm.

down

up

UTIL.
8-4 x 5-8
w d

8-8 x 13-2

sto.

sto.

PORCH

GARAGE
22-0 x 34-0

LOWER LEVEL

PATIO

UNFINISHED
STORAGE/
MECHANICAL
13-4 x 15-8

fireplace

FAMILY RM.
17-10 x 15-6

wet bar

BED RM./
STUDY
12-2 x 10-2

bath

sto.

plan #

HPT9800113

STYLE: CRAFTSMAN
MAIN LEVEL: 1,662 SQ. FT.
UPPER LEVEL: 585 SQ. FT.
LOWER LEVEL: 706 SQ. FT.
TOTAL: 2,953 SQ. FT.
BONUS SPACE: 575 SQ. FT.
BEDROOMS: 4
BATHROOMS: 3½
WIDTH: 81' - 4"
DEPTH: 68' - 8"

SEARCH ONLINE @ EPLANS.COM

A stunning center dormer with an arched window embellishes the exterior of this Craftsman-style home. The dormer's arched window allows light into the foyer and built-in niche. The second-floor hall is a balcony that overlooks both the foyer and great room. A generous back porch extends the great room, which features an impressive vaulted ceiling and fireplace; a tray ceiling adorns the formal dining room. The master suite, which includes a tray ceiling as well, enjoys back-porch access, a built-in cabinet, generous walk-in closet, and private bath. Two more bedrooms are located upstairs; a fourth can be found in the lower level along with a family room.

REAR EXTERIOR

© 1998 Donald A. Gardner, Inc.

plan

HPT9800009

STYLE: BUNGALOW
FIRST FLOOR: 1,661 SQ. FT.
SECOND FLOOR: 882 SQ. FT.
TOTAL: 2,543 SQ. FT.
BEDROOMS: 3
BATHROOMS: 3½
WIDTH: 59' - 0"
DEPTH: 58' - 11"
FOUNDATION: CRAWLSPACE

SEARCH ONLINE @ EPLANS.COM

With rustic rafter tails, sturdy pillars, and a siding-and-shingle facade, this welcoming bungalow offers plenty of curb appeal. Inside, the formal dining room sits to the left of the foyer and gives easy access to the angled kitchen. A spacious gathering room offers a fireplace, built-ins, a wall of windows, and access to a covered terrace. Located on the first floor for privacy, the master bedroom is lavish with its amenities, including His and Hers walk-in closets and basins, a garden tub, and a compartmented toilet. Upstairs, two suites offer private baths and share a linkside retreat that includes a fairway veranda.

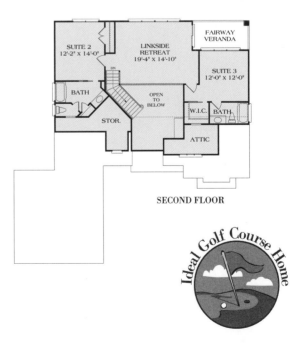

SECOND FLOOR

FIRST FLOOR

Ideal Golf Course Home

Quaint keystones and shutters offer charming accents to the stucco-and-stone exterior of this stately English Country home. The two-story foyer opens through decorative columns to the formal living room, which offers a wet bar. The nearby media room shares a through-fireplace with the two-story great room, which has double doors that lead to the rear deck. A bumped-out bay holds a breakfast area that shares its light with an expansive cooktop-island kitchen. This area opens to the formal dining room through a convenient butler's pantry. One wing of the second floor is dedicated to the rambling master suite, which boasts unusual amenities with angled walls, a tray ceiling, and a bumped-out bay with a sitting area in the bedroom.

plan
HPT9800114

STYLE: COUNTRY COTTAGE
FIRST FLOOR: 1,475 SQ. FT.
SECOND FLOOR: 1,460 SQ. FT.
TOTAL: 2,935 SQ. FT.
BEDROOMS: 4
BATHROOMS: 3½
WIDTH: 57' - 6"
DEPTH: 46' - 6"
FOUNDATION: WALKOUT BASEMENT

SEARCH ONLINE @ EPLANS.COM

QUOTE ONE®
Cost to build? See page 187 to order complete cost estimate to build this house in your area!

FIRST FLOOR

SECOND FLOOR

plan
HPT9800115

STYLE: TRADITIONAL
SQUARE FOOTAGE: 2,663
BONUS SPACE: 653 SQ. FT.
BEDROOMS: 4
BATHROOMS: 2½
WIDTH: 72' - 7"
DEPTH: 78' - 0"

SEARCH ONLINE @ EPLANS.COM

REAR EXTERIOR

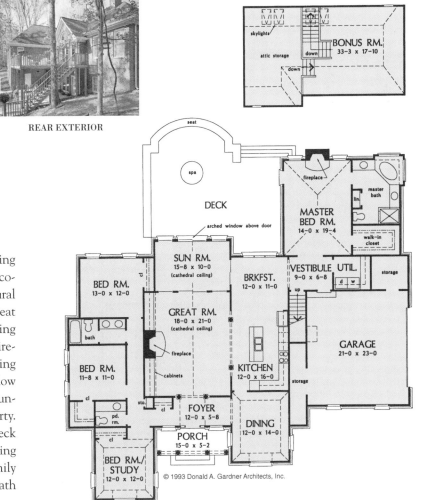

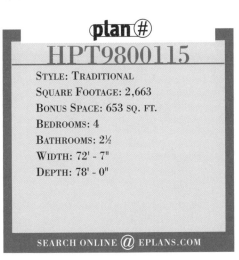

This home's personality is reflected in charming arch-top windows, set off with keystones and decorative shutters. A columned foyer enjoys natural light from a clerestory window and opens to the great room, which boasts a cathedral ceiling and sliding glass doors to the sunroom. An extended-hearth fireplace adds warmth to the living area. Open planning allows the nearby gourmet kitchen to share the glow of the hearth. The breakfast room really lets the sunshine in with a triple window to the rear property. The master suite offers private access to the rear deck with a spa and features a cozy fireplace, a relaxing bath, and a generous walk-in closet. Three family bedrooms—or make one a study—share a full bath and a powder room on the other side of the plan.

© 1993 Donald A. Gardner Architects, Inc.

Mixed materials and a front covered porch highlight the exterior of this lovely home. The two-story foyer is flanked on either side by the study and dining room. The vaulted family room features a fireplace and built-ins. The master suite is located on the first floor for privacy and includes a vaulted bath and a roomy walk-in closet. Three additional bedrooms and an optional bonus room are located on the second floor.

plan #

HPT9800116

STYLE: COUNTRY COTTAGE
FIRST FLOOR: 1,969 SQ. FT.
SECOND FLOOR: 894 SQ. FT.
TOTAL: 2,863 SQ. FT.
BONUS SPACE: 213 SQ. FT.
BEDROOMS: 4
BATHROOMS: 2½
WIDTH: 55' - 0"
DEPTH: 54' - 0"
FOUNDATION: BASEMENT, CRAWLSPACE

SEARCH ONLINE @ EPLANS.COM

FIRST FLOOR

SECOND FLOOR

plan

HPT9800117

STYLE: TRANSITIONAL
FIRST FLOOR: 2,192 SQ. FT.
SECOND FLOOR: 654 SQ. FT.
TOTAL: 2,846 SQ. FT.
BONUS SPACE: 325 SQ. FT.
BEDROOMS: 3
BATHROOMS: 2½ + ½
WIDTH: 74' - 4"
DEPTH: 69' - 11"
FOUNDATION: BASEMENT

SEARCH ONLINE @ EPLANS.COM

Multiple gables, a box window, and keystone lintels combine to create a dramatic appearance for this European classic home. The excitement of the great room begins with a wall of windows, sloped ceiling, and built-in entertainment cabinet. The kitchen offers an angled island that parallels the French doors and a large breakfast room. The luxury and convenience of the first-floor master bedroom suite is highlighted by His and Hers vanities, a shower, and a whirlpool tub. The second floor provides a private retreat for a guest suite and a bonus room, which offers the option of a fourth bedroom, a library, or hobby room.

SECOND FLOOR

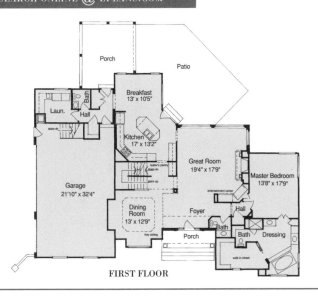

FIRST FLOOR

This engaging home is inspired by French eclectic architecture with striking style. A formal entry presents the dining room on the left, defined by stately columns. French doors open to the study, a quiet place for contemplation. Continue to the two-story family room, lit by tall windows and warmed by a fireplace. Rear-veranda access near the kitchen and breakfast nook encourages alfresco dining. Sloped ceilings in the master suite are emphasized by a Palladian window; a private bath will pamper and soothe. Upstairs, three bedrooms are generously appointed. Optional attic space provides plenty of room for storage.

plan#

HPT9800118

STYLE: TRADITIONAL
FIRST FLOOR: 1,844 SQ. FT.
SECOND FLOOR: 794 SQ. FT.
TOTAL: 2,638 SQ. FT.
BEDROOMS: 4
BATHROOMS: 3½
WIDTH: 65' - 6"
DEPTH: 56' - 10"

SEARCH ONLINE @ EPLANS.COM

FIRST FLOOR

SECOND FLOOR

plan #

HPT9800119

STYLE: TRADITIONAL

SQUARE FOOTAGE: 2,985

BEDROOMS: 4

BATHROOMS: 3½

WIDTH: 80' - 0"

DEPTH: 68' - 0"

FOUNDATION: SLAB

SEARCH ONLINE @ EPLANS.COM

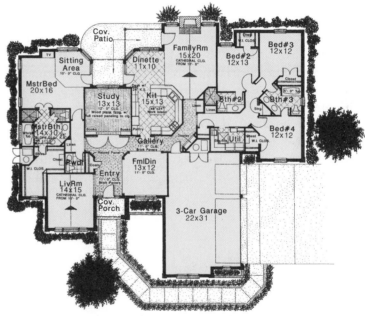

A brick exterior, cast-stone trim, and corner quoins make up this attractive single-living-area design. The entry introduces a formal dining room to the right and a living room with a wall of windows to the left. The hearth-warmed family room opens to the kitchen/dinette, both with 10-foot ceilings. A large bay window enhances the dinette with a full glass door to the covered patio. A large master suite with vaulted ceilings features a bayed sitting area, a luxurious bath with double sinks, and an oversize walk-in closet.

ALTERNATE EXTERIOR

European details highlight this attractive compact exterior. Note the double-brick arches over the windows and entry, the wooden shutters, and the stone exterior. The two-story foyer opens to a wide hallway with a coat closet and an elegant stairway. To the left, the den (or living room) features an unusual window and built-in cabinets. The dining room is to the right, just a short trip from the kitchen. Here, the family chef will appreciate a work island/snack bar combination, a walk-in pantry, and a corner window sink. A bayed nook offers access to a screened porch. There's also a covered porch off the great room, which has an impressive fireplace flanked by cabinets. The master suite pampers with two closets, a garden tub, and a dual-bowl vanity.

plan #

HPT9800120

STYLE: COUNTRY COTTAGE
FIRST FLOOR: 2,172 SQ. FT.
SECOND FLOOR: 690 SQ. FT.
TOTAL: 2,862 SQ. FT.
BONUS SPACE: 450 SQ. FT.
BEDROOMS: 4
BATHROOMS: 2½
WIDTH: 72' - 0"
DEPTH: 73' - 0"
FOUNDATION: BASEMENT

SEARCH ONLINE @ EPLANS.COM

FIRST FLOOR

SECOND FLOOR

plan #

HPT9800121

STYLE: TRADITIONAL

SQUARE FOOTAGE: 2,696

BEDROOMS: 4

BATHROOMS: 3½

WIDTH: 80' - 0"

DEPTH: 64' - 1"

FOUNDATION: SLAB

SEARCH ONLINE @ EPLANS.COM

A brick archway covers the front porch of this European-style home, creating a truly grand entrance. Situated beyond the entry, the living room takes center stage with a fireplace flanked by tall windows. To the right is a bayed eating area and an efficient kitchen. Steps away is the formal dining room. Skillful planning creates flexibility for the master suite. If you wish, use Bedroom 2 as a secondary bedroom or guest room, with the adjacent study accessible to everyone. Or if you prefer, combine the master suite with the study and use it as a private retreat with Bedroom 2 as a nursery, creating a wing that provides complete privacy. Completing this clever plan are two family bedrooms, a powder room, and a utility room.

Wood shingles are a cozy touch on the exterior of this home. Interior rooms include a great room with a fireplace, a formal dining room, and a study with another fireplace. A guest room on the first floor contains a full bath and walk-in closet. The master bedroom is also on the first floor for privacy. The second floor holds two additional bedrooms, a loft area and a gallery overlooking the central hall.

ptan#

HPT9800122

STYLE: COUNTRY COTTAGE
FIRST FLOOR: 2,070 SQ. FT.
SECOND FLOOR: 790 SQ. FT.
TOTAL: 2,860 SQ. FT.
BEDROOMS: 4
BATHROOMS: 3½
WIDTH: 57' - 6"
DEPTH: 54' - 0"
FOUNDATION: WALKOUT BASEMENT

SEARCH ONLINE @ EPLANS.COM

SECOND FLOOR

FIRST FLOOR

REAR EXTERIOR

plan
HPT9800123

STYLE: EUROPEAN COTTAGE
FIRST FLOOR: 1,862 SQ. FT.
SECOND FLOOR: 1,044 SQ. FT.
TOTAL: 2,906 SQ. FT.
BONUS SPACE: 259 SQ. FT.
BEDROOMS: 3
BATHROOMS: 3½
WIDTH: 60' - 0"
DEPTH: 60' - 0"
FOUNDATION: CRAWLSPACE

SEARCH ONLINE @ EPLANS.COM

A gently sloping, high-pitched roof complements keystones, arch-top windows, and a delicate balcony balustrade, calling up a sense of cozy elegance. The foyer opens to a grand room with a focal-point fireplace and access to a screened room that leads to the veranda. The gourmet kitchen offers a walk-in pantry, acres of counter space, and a morning room with outdoor flow. An island wardrobe highlights the master suite, which boasts a secluded lounge with a door to a private area of the veranda. Upstairs, two secondary bedrooms enjoy a balcony overlook to the foyer, and each room has its own access to an outdoor deck.

SECOND FLOOR

FIRST FLOOR

This exquisite European cottage offers all the charm of the Old World. A beautiful courtyard announces your entry. The foyer is flanked by a dining room and study. The kitchen features a snack counter, while the nook extends double-door access to the three-season porch. The master suite includes a pampering private bath and walk-in closet. A three-car garage completes the first floor. Three family bedrooms reside upstairs.

ptan #

HPT9800124

STYLE: COUNTRY COTTAGE
FIRST FLOOR: 2,079 SQ. FT.
SECOND FLOOR: 796 SQ. FT.
TOTAL: 2,875 SQ. FT.
BEDROOMS: 4
BATHROOMS: 2½
WIDTH: 63' - 0"
DEPTH: 68' - 0"
FOUNDATION: BASEMENT

SEARCH ONLINE @ EPLANS.COM

FIRST FLOOR

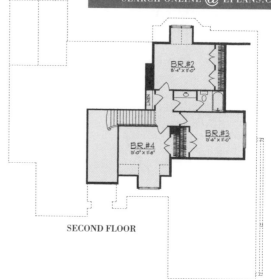

SECOND FLOOR

plan

HPT9800040

STYLE: EUROPEAN COTTAGE
FIRST FLOOR: 1,395 SQ. FT.
SECOND FLOOR: 1,210 SQ. FT.
TOTAL: 2,605 SQ. FT.
BONUS SPACE: 225 SQ. FT.
BEDROOMS: 3
BATHROOMS: 2½
WIDTH: 47' - 0"
DEPTH: 49' - 6"
FOUNDATION: BASEMENT

SEARCH ONLINE @ EPLANS.COM

The well-balanced use of stucco and stone combined with box-bay window treatments and a covered entry make this English Country home especially inviting. The two-story foyer opens on the right to formal living and dining rooms, bright with natural light. A spacious U-shaped kitchen adjoins a breakfast nook with views of the outdoors. This area flows nicely into the two-story great room, which offers a through-fireplace to the media room. A plush retreat awaits the homeowner upstairs with a master suite that offers a quiet, windowed sitting area with views to the rear grounds. Two family bedrooms share a full bath and a balcony hall that has a dramatic view of the great room below.

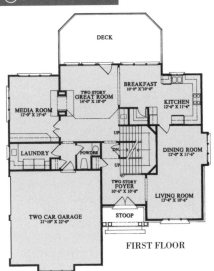

FIRST FLOOR

SECOND FLOOR

QUOTE ONE®
Cost to build? See page 187
to order complete cost estimate
to build this house in your area!

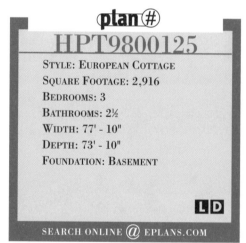

plan #

HPT9800125

STYLE: EUROPEAN COTTAGE

SQUARE FOOTAGE: 2,916

BEDROOMS: 3

BATHROOMS: 2½

WIDTH: 77' - 10"

DEPTH: 73' - 10"

FOUNDATION: BASEMENT

L D

SEARCH ONLINE @ EPLANS.COM

Intricate details make the most of this lovely one-story design. Besides the living room/dining room combination to the rear, there is a large conversation area with a fireplace and plenty of windows. The kitchen is separated from the living areas by an angled snack-bar counter. Three bedrooms grace the right side of the plan. The master suite features a tray ceiling and sliding glass doors to the rear terrace. The dressing area is graced by His and Hers walk-in closets, a double-bowl vanity, and a compartmented toilet. The sunken shower area is highlighted with glass block. A garden whirlpool tub finishes off this area.

Quote One®

Cost to build? See page 187
to order complete cost estimate
to build this house in your area!

Great for a Mountainside Lot

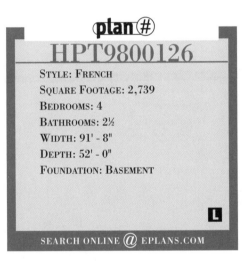

plan #

HPT9800126

STYLE: FRENCH

SQUARE FOOTAGE: 2,739

BEDROOMS: 4

BATHROOMS: 2½

WIDTH: 91' - 8"

DEPTH: 52' - 0"

FOUNDATION: BASEMENT

L

SEARCH ONLINE @ EPLANS.COM

Quote One®

Cost to build? See page 187
to order complete cost estimate
to build this house in your area!

This spacious one-story home has a classic French Country hipped roof. Beyond the covered porch is an octagonal foyer. All of the living areas overlook the rear yard. Features include a fireplace in the living room, a skylight in the dining room, and a second set of sliding glass doors in the family room leading to a covered porch. An island cooktop and other built-ins are featured in the roomy kitchen. Adjacent is the breakfast room, which can be used for informal dining. The four bedrooms and the baths are clustered in one wing. Bay windows brighten the master bedroom, the breakfast room, and the three-car garage.

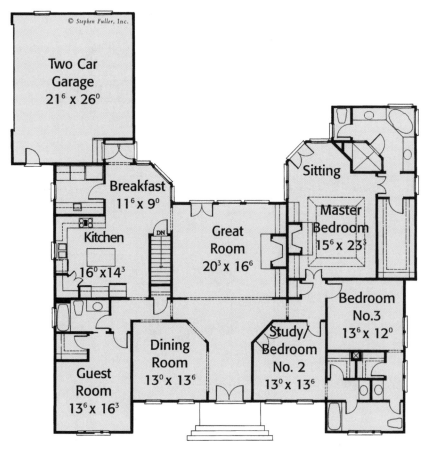

© Stephen Fuller, Inc.

Two Car Garage 21⁶ x 26⁰

Breakfast 11⁶ x 9⁰

Kitchen 16⁰ x 14³

Great Room 20³ x 16⁶

Sitting

Master Bedroom 15⁶ x 23³

Bedroom No.3 13⁶ x 12⁰

Dining Room 13⁰ x 13⁶

Study/ Bedroom No. 2 13⁰ x 13⁶

Guest Room 13⁶ x 16³

plan #
HPT9800127

STYLE: CONTEMPORARY
SQUARE FOOTAGE: 2,785
BEDROOMS: 4
BATHROOMS: 3
WIDTH: 72' - 0"
DEPTH: 72' - 0"
FOUNDATION: BASEMENT

SEARCH ONLINE @ EPLANS.COM

This elegant Colonial design boasts many European influences such as the stucco facade, corner quoins, and arched windows. The foyer is flanked by a formal dining room and a study, which converts to an additional bedroom. Straight ahead, the great room, featuring a fireplace and built-ins, accesses the rear yard. The island kitchen opens to a breakfast nook for casual occasions. The master suite on the opposite side of the home boasts wondrous amenities such as a private fireplace, a bayed sitting area accessing the rear, a lavish bath, and an enormous walk-in closet.

plan #

HPT9800128

STYLE: ITALIANATE

FIRST FLOOR: 2,096 SQ. FT.

SECOND FLOOR: 892 SQ. FT.

TOTAL: 2,988 SQ. FT.

BEDROOMS: 3

BATHROOMS: 3½

WIDTH: 56' - 0"

DEPTH: 54' - 0"

FOUNDATION: BASEMENT

SEARCH ONLINE @ EPLANS.COM

Multiple windows bring natural light to this beautiful home, which offers a floor plan filled with special amenities. Arches provide a grand entry to the beam-ceilinged great room, where built-ins flank the fireplace and three sets of French doors open to a veranda. Stepped ceilings grace the master suite and the dining room. The master suite provides two walk-in closets and a resplendent bath, while dazzling windows in the dining room allow enjoyment of the outdoors. Two second-floor bedrooms, one with a sundeck, feature walk-in closets and private baths.

SECOND FLOOR

FIRST FLOOR

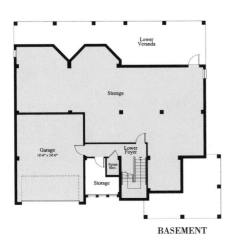

BASEMENT

Perfect Waterfront Plan

Clean, contemporary lines, a unique floor plan, and a metal roof with a cupola set this farmhouse apart. Remote-control transoms in the cupola open to create an airy and decidedly unique foyer. The great room, sunroom, dining room, and kitchen flow from one to another for casual entertaining with flair. The rear of the home is fashioned with plenty of windows overlooking the multilevel deck. A front bedroom and bath would make a comfortable guest suite. The master bedroom and bath upstairs are bridged by a pipe-rail balcony that also gives access to a rear deck. An additional bedroom, home office, and bath complete this very special plan.

plan#

HPT9800129

STYLE: CONTEMPORARY
FIRST FLOOR: 1,309 SQ. FT.
SECOND FLOOR: 1,343 SQ. FT.
TOTAL: 2,652 SQ. FT.
BEDROOMS: 3
BATHROOMS: 3
WIDTH: 44' - 4"
DEPTH: 58' - 2"
FOUNDATION: CRAWLSPACE

SEARCH ONLINE @ EPLANS.COM

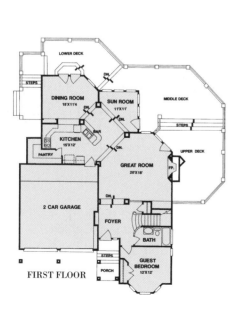

FIRST FLOOR

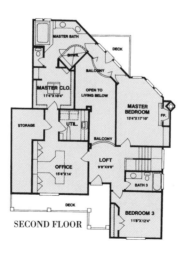

SECOND FLOOR

REAR EXTERIOR

plan

HPT9800130

STYLE: FLORIDIAN

FIRST FLOOR: 2,066 SQ. FT.

SECOND FLOOR: 810 SQ. FT.

TOTAL: 2,876 SQ. FT.

BONUS SPACE: 1,260 SQ. FT.

BEDROOMS: 3

BATHROOMS: 3½

WIDTH: 64' - 0"

DEPTH: 45' - 0"

FOUNDATION: PIER

L

SEARCH ONLINE @ EPLANS.COM

If entertaining is your passion, then this is the design for you. With a large, open floor plan and an array of amenities, every gathering will be a success. The foyer embraces living areas accented by a glass fireplace and a wet bar. The grand room and dining room each access a screened veranda for outside enjoyments. The gourmet kitchen delights with its openness to the rest of the house. A morning nook here also adds a nice touch. Two bedrooms and a study radiate from the first-floor living areas. Upstairs—or use the elevator—is a masterful master suite. It contains a huge walk-in closet, a whirlpool tub, and a private sundeck with a spa.

SECOND FLOOR

FIRST FLOOR

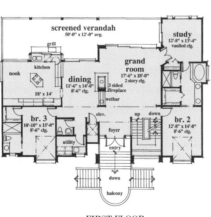

BASEMENT

REAR EXTERIOR

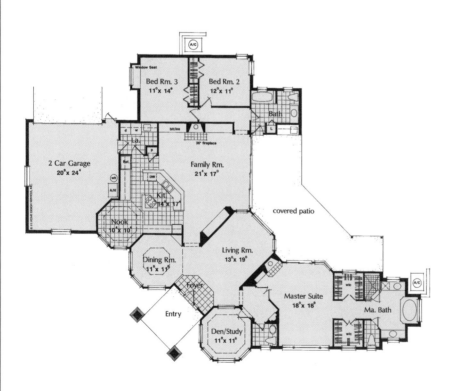

ptan #

HPT9800131

STYLE: FLORIDIAN
SQUARE FOOTAGE: 2,656
BEDROOMS: 3
BATHROOMS: 2½
WIDTH: 92' - 0"
DEPTH: 69' - 0"
FOUNDATION: SLAB

SEARCH ONLINE @ EPLANS.COM

A graceful design sets this charming home apart from the ordinary and transcends the commonplace. From the foyer, the dining room branches off the sunny living room, setting a lovely backdrop for entertaining. Casual living is the focus in the oversized family room, where sliding doors open to the patio and the eat-in, gourmet kitchen is open for easy conversation. Two family bedrooms and a cabana bath are just off the family room. The master suite has a cozy fireplace in the sitting area, twin closets, and a compartmented bath. A large covered patio adds to the living area.

plan ⊕

HPT9800132

STYLE: ITALIANATE
FIRST FLOOR: 1,266 SQ. FT.
SECOND FLOOR: 1,324 SQ. FT.
TOTAL: 2,590 SQ. FT.
BEDROOMS: 3
BATHROOMS: 2½
WIDTH: 34' - 0"
DEPTH: 63' - 2"
FOUNDATION: SLAB

SEARCH ONLINE @ EPLANS.COM

This modern take on the Italian villa boasts plenty of indoor/outdoor flow. Four sets of double doors wrap around the great room and dining area and open to the stunning veranda. The great room is enhanced by a coffered ceiling and built-in cabinetry, and the entire first floor is bathed in sunlight from a wall of glass doors overlooking the veranda. The dining room connects to a gourmet island kitchen. Upstairs, a beautiful deck wraps gracefully around the family bedrooms. The master suite is a skylit haven enhanced by a sitting bay, which features a vaulted octagonal ceiling and a cozy two-sided fireplace. Private double doors access the sundeck from the master suite, the secondary bedrooms, and the study.

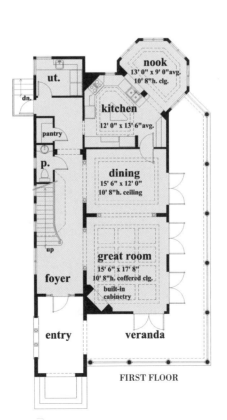

FIRST FLOOR

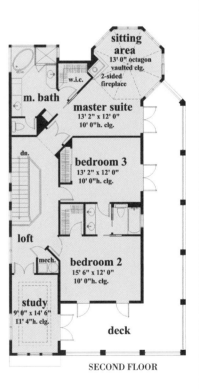

SECOND FLOOR

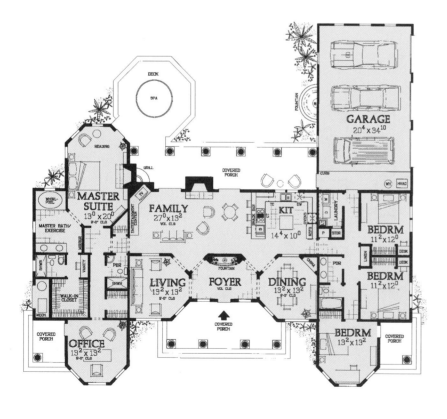

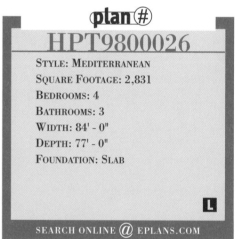

plan #

HPT9800026

STYLE: Mediterranean

SQUARE FOOTAGE: 2,831

BEDROOMS: 4

BATHROOMS: 3

WIDTH: 84' - 0"

DEPTH: 77' - 0"

FOUNDATION: Slab

SEARCH ONLINE @ EPLANS.COM

Besides great curb appeal, this home has a wonderful floor plan. The foyer features a fountain that greets visitors and leads to a formal dining room on the right and a living room on the left. A large family room at the rear has a built-in entertainment center and a fireplace. The U-shaped kitchen is perfectly located for servicing all living and dining areas. To the right of the plan, away from the central entertaining spaces, are three family bedrooms sharing a full bath. On the left side, with solitude and comfort for the master suite, are a large sitting area, an office, and an amenity-filled bath. A deck with a spa sits outside the master suite.

plan #

HPT9800038

STYLE: COUNTRY COTTAGE
FIRST FLOOR: 2,086 SQ. FT.
SECOND FLOOR: 1,077 SQ. FT.
TOTAL: 3,163 SQ. FT.
BONUS SPACE: 403 SQ. FT.
BEDROOMS: 4
BATHROOMS: 3½
WIDTH: 81' - 10"
DEPTH: 51' - 8"

SEARCH ONLINE @ EPLANS.COM

This beautiful farmhouse, with its prominent twin gables and bays, adds just the right amount of country style. The master suite is quietly tucked away downstairs with no rooms directly above. The family cook will love the spacious U-shaped kitchen and adjoining bayed breakfast nook. A bonus room awaits expansion on the second floor, where three large bedrooms share two full baths. Storage space abounds with walk-ins, half-shelves, and linen closets. A curved balcony borders a versatile loft/study, which overlooks the stunning two-story family room.

SECOND FLOOR

FIRST FLOOR

REAR EXTERIOR

A prominent center gable with an arched window accents the facade of this custom Craftsman home, which features an exterior of cedar shakes, siding, and stone. An open floor plan with generously proportioned rooms contributes to the spacious and relaxed atmosphere. The vaulted great room boasts a rear wall of windows, a fireplace bordered by built-in cabinets, and convenient access to the kitchen. A second-floor loft overlooks the great room for added drama. The master suite is completely secluded and enjoys a cathedral ceiling, back-porch access, a large walk-in closet, and a luxurious bath. The home includes three additional bedrooms and baths as well as a vaulted loft/study and a bonus room.

plan #

HPT9800032

STYLE: CRAFTSMAN
FIRST FLOOR: 2,477 SQ. FT.
SECOND FLOOR: 742 SQ. FT.
TOTAL: 3,219 SQ. FT.
BONUS SPACE: 419 SQ. FT.
BEDROOMS: 4
BATHROOMS: 4
WIDTH: 100' - 0"
DEPTH: 66' - 2"

SEARCH ONLINE @ EPLANS.COM

FIRST FLOOR

BRKFST. 12-0 x 12-0 (vaulted ceiling)
PORCH
MASTER BED RM. 16-0 x 18-0 (cathedral ceiling)
walk-in closet
DECK
KITCHEN 13-0 x 13-2
GREAT RM. 22-8 x 17-0 (vaulted ceiling)
fireplace
balcony above
master bath
UTIL. 13-0 x 8-4
DINING 15-4 x 12-0
FOYER 8-0 x 12-0
up
bath
GARAGE 22-0 x 23-4
BED RM./ STUDY 13-0 x 14-0 (cathedral ceiling)
PORCH
© 1999 DAC All rights reserved

Great for a Mountainside Lot

SECOND FLOOR

great room below
BED RM. 13-0 x 11-0
bath
BED RM. 12-8 x 11-0
walk-in closet
railing
down
walk-in closet
bath
LOFT/ STUDY 10-4 x 12-4 (vaulted ceiling)
attic storage
BONUS RM. 12-0 x 23-4
attic storage

ptan #

HPT9800133

STYLE: VACATION
FIRST FLOOR: 1,437 SQ. FT.
SECOND FLOOR: 1,635 SQ. FT.
TOTAL: 3,072 SQ. FT.
BEDROOMS: 4
BATHROOMS: 3
WIDTH: 62' - 0"
DEPTH: 36' - 0"
FOUNDATION: BASEMENT

SEARCH ONLINE @ EPLANS.COM

This beautiful chalet vacation home abounds with views of the outdoors and provides a grand deck, creating additional living space. With its entry on the lower level, you'll find two family bedrooms that share a full bath, an office/study, and a family room with a warming fireplace. There's an extra room here that could be a third family bedroom or perhaps a library or study. Upstairs, a great room with a cathedral ceiling shares a through-fireplace with the formal dining room. Conveniently nearby is the kitchen, which boasts an island work area/snack bar and an informal dining area. Also on this upper level is the master suite with its own private bath. A fourth bedroom and another full bath will certainly accommodate weekend or overnight guests.

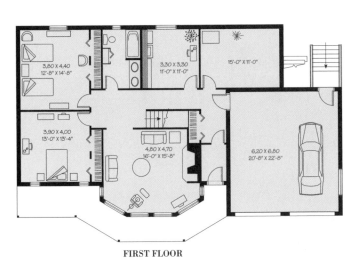

FIRST FLOOR

SECOND FLOOR

©1998 Donald A. Gardner, Inc.

Stone, siding, and multiple gables combine beautifully on the exterior of this hillside home. Taking advantage of rear views, the home's most oft-used rooms are oriented at the back with plenty of windows. Augmented by a cathedral ceiling, the great room features a fireplace, built-in shelves, and access to the rear deck. Twin walk-in closets and a private bath infuse the master suite with luxury. The nearby powder room offers an optional full-bath arrangement, allowing the study to double as a bedroom. Downstairs, a large media/recreation room with a wet bar and fireplace separates two more bedrooms, each with a full bath and walk-in closet.

plan#
HPT9800134

STYLE: BUNGALOW
MAIN LEVEL: 2,065 SQ. FT.
LOWER LEVEL: 1,216 SQ. FT.
TOTAL: 3,281 SQ. FT.
BEDROOMS: 4
BATHROOMS: 3½
WIDTH: 82' - 2"
DEPTH: 43' - 6"

SEARCH ONLINE @ EPLANS.COM

LOWER LEVEL

REAR EXTERIOR

MAIN LEVEL

© 1998 Donald A Gardner, Inc.

ptan#

HPT9800135

STYLE: FARMHOUSE

FIRST FLOOR: 2,191 SQ. FT.

SECOND FLOOR: 1,220 SQ. FT.

TOTAL: 3,411 SQ. FT.

BONUS SPACE: 280 SQ. FT.

BEDROOMS: 4

BATHROOMS: 3½

WIDTH: 75' - 8"

DEPTH: 54' - 4"

FOUNDATION: BASEMENT, CRAWLSPACE, SLAB

SEARCH ONLINE @ EPLANS.COM

This Colonial farmhouse will be the showpiece of your neighborhood. Come in from the wide front porch through French doors topped by a sunburst window. Continue past the formal dining and living rooms to a columned gallery and a large family room with a focal fireplace. The kitchen astounds with a unique layout, an island, and abundant counter and cabinet space. The master bath balances luxury with efficiency. Three upstairs bedrooms enjoy amenities such as dormer windows or walk-in closets. Bonus space is ready for expansion as your needs change.

FIRST FLOOR

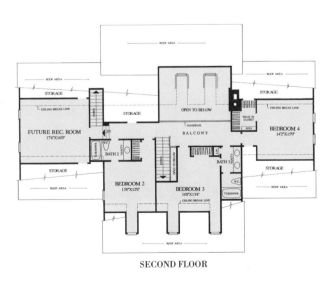

SECOND FLOOR

This Colonial ranch house was built with luxury in mind. Enter past the powder room and coat closet to the family room with a two-story ceiling and focal-point fireplace. The angled kitchen provides room to move and lots of counter space. The real star of the home is the dazzling master suite. Running the depth of the home, this sanctuary features natural light, a stunning bath with a "boomerang" twin vanity, and a walk-in closet with window seats to impress any fashion connoisseur. Two complete suites and room to expand finish the plan.

plan #

HPT9800136

STYLE: COLONIAL
FIRST FLOOR: 2,335 SQ. FT.
SECOND FLOOR: 936 SQ. FT.
TOTAL: 3,271 SQ. FT.
BONUS SPACE: 958 SQ. FT.
BEDROOMS: 3
BATHROOMS: 3½
WIDTH: 91' - 4"
DEPTH: 54' - 6"
FOUNDATION: BASEMENT

SEARCH ONLINE @ EPLANS.COM

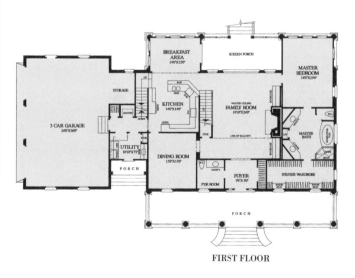

FIRST FLOOR

SECOND FLOOR

plan #

HPT9800137

STYLE: FARMHOUSE

FIRST FLOOR: 2,347 SQ. FT.

SECOND FLOOR: 1,087 SQ. FT.

TOTAL: 3,434 SQ. FT.

BEDROOMS: 4

BATHROOMS: 2½

WIDTH: 93' - 6"

DEPTH: 61' - 0"

FOUNDATION: BASEMENT

SEARCH ONLINE @ EPLANS.COM

Dutch-gable rooflines and a gabled wraparound porch provide an extra measure of farmhouse style. The foyer opens on the left to the study or guest bedroom that leads to the master suite. To the right is the formal dining room; the massive great room is in the center. The kitchen combines with the great room, the breakfast nook, and the dining room for entertaining options. The master suite includes access to the covered patio, a spacious walk-in closet, and a full bath with a whirlpool tub.

SECOND FLOOR

QUOTE ONE®

Cost to build? See page 187
to order complete cost estimate
to build this house in your area!

FIRST FLOOR

Hipped rooflines, flower boxes, and shed-style dormers serve to distinguish this home. Both the dining room and the master suite are graced with tray ceilings, lending a sense of increased spaciousness to the plan. The great room resides on the right side of the plan and boasts a corner fireplace, an abundance of windows, and access to a side deck. The U-shaped kitchen—complete with a cooktop island—nestles close to the bayed breakfast area and the first-floor powder room. Four family suites make up the second level. Suites 2 and 4 are graced with bay windows and a walk-through bath. Suites 3 and 5 share a hall bath. A laundry area is located conveniently near these bedrooms for easy washing.

plan #

HPT9800002

STYLE: EUROPEAN COTTAGE
FIRST FLOOR: 1,790 SQ. FT.
SECOND FLOOR: 1,484 SQ. FT.
TOTAL: 3,274 SQ. FT.
BEDROOMS: 5
BATHROOMS: 3½
WIDTH: 67' - 0"
DEPTH: 44' - 8"
FOUNDATION: BASEMENT

SEARCH ONLINE @ EPLANS.COM

© 1999 Donald A. Gardner, Inc.

plan
HPT9800018

STYLE: CONTEMPORARY
MAIN LEVEL: 2,122 SQ. FT.
LOWER LEVEL: 1,290 SQ. FT.
TOTAL: 3,412 SQ. FT.
BEDROOMS: 4
BATHROOMS: 3
WIDTH: 83' - 0"
DEPTH: 74' - 4"

SEARCH ONLINE @ EPLANS.COM

A Craftsman combination of cedar shingles and wood siding lends warmth and style to this four-bedroom home. A stunning cathedral ceiling spans the open great room and spaciousisland kitchen for exceptional volume. A deep tray ceiling heightens the formal dining room, while the breakfast room is enhanced by a vaulted ceiling. Two rear decks and a screened porch augment the home's ample living space. The master bedroom is topped by a tray ceiling and features two walk-in closets and a generous private bath. A second bedroom is located on the main leveland two more can be found on the lower level.

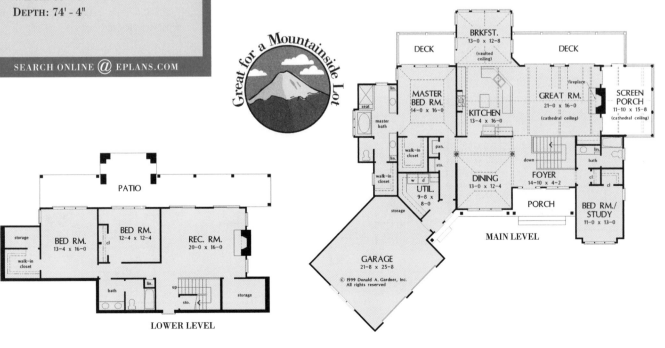

Tall windows wrap this noble exterior with dazzling details and allow plenty of natural light inside. A wraparound porch sets a casual but elegant pace for the home, with space for rockers and swings. Well-defined formal rooms are placed just off the foyer. A host of French doors opens the great room to an entertainment porch and, of course, inspiring views. Even formal meals take on the ease and comfort of a mountain region in the stunning open dining room. Nearby, a gourmet kitchen packed with amenities serves any occasion.

plan #

HPT9800019

STYLE: BUNGALOW
FIRST FLOOR: 2,146 SQ. FT.
SECOND FLOOR: 952 SQ. FT.
TOTAL: 3,098 SQ. FT.
BEDROOMS: 3
BATHROOMS: 3½
WIDTH: 52' - 0"
DEPTH: 65' - 4"
FOUNDATION: BASEMENT

SEARCH ONLINE @ EPLANS.COM

BASEMENT

- up
- porch
- 2 car garage — 9' 0"h. ceiling
- storage/ bonus room — 8' 8"h. ceiling
- mud room
- up
- vest.
- ski stor. — 8' 8"h. ceiling

FIRST FLOOR

- dn.
- porch
- nook — 14' 0" x 9' 0" avg. 10' 0"h. clg.
- great room — 20' 4" x 18' 4" 2 story clg.
- built-in cabinetry
- master suite — 14' 0" x 14' 0" avg. 10' 0"h. clg.
- kitchen — 14' 0" x 15' 0" 10' 0"h. clg.
- fireplace
- built-in cabinetry
- wet bar
- utility
- dn.
- linen
- dining — 13' 0" x 14' 3" 12' 4"h. clg.
- foyer
- study — 13' 0" x 12' 0" 12' 4"h. clg.
- entry porch

SECOND FLOOR

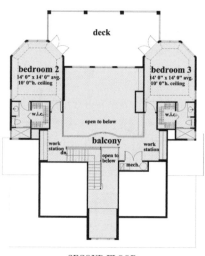

- deck
- bedroom 2 — 14' 0" x 14' 0" avg. 10' 0"h. ceiling
- bedroom 3 — 14' 0" x 14' 0" avg. 10' 0"h. ceiling
- w.i.c.
- w.i.c.
- open to below
- work station
- balcony
- work station
- dn.
- open to below
- mech.

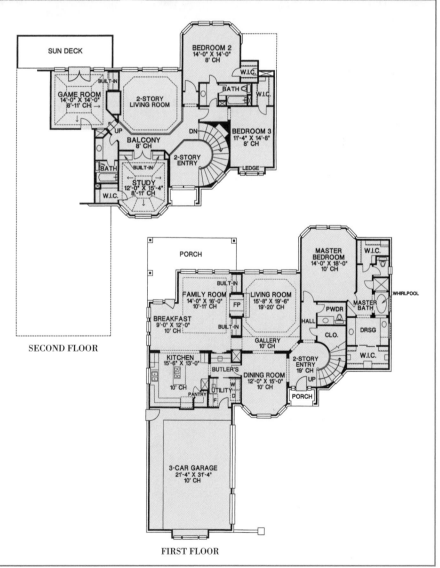

plan

HPT9800029

STYLE: COLONIAL
FIRST FLOOR: 2,144 SQ. FT.
SECOND FLOOR: 1,253 SQ. FT.
TOTAL: 3,397 SQ. FT.
BEDROOMS: 3
BATHROOMS: 3½
WIDTH: 64' - 11"
DEPTH: 76' - 7"

SEARCH ONLINE @ EPLANS.COM

This two-story beauty is rich in luxurious style. A dramatic entrance welcomes you to the foyer, where a stunning curved staircase greets you. A turret-style dining room is flooded with light from the bayed windows. Across the gallery, the living room features a through-fireplace to the family room. The island kitchen is open to the breakfast room, which accesses the rear porch and the family room equipped with built-ins. The first-floor master bedroom offers a bath with a whirlpool tub, two walk-in closets, and a dressing room. Two additional bedrooms, a study, and a game room with sundeck access all reside on the second floor.

SECOND FLOOR

FIRST FLOOR

The grand exterior of this Normandy country design features a steeply pitched gable roofline. Arched dormers repeat the window accents. Inside, the promise of space is fulfilled with a large gathering room that fills the center of the house and opens to a long trellised veranda. The den or guest suite with a fireplace, the adjacent powder room, and the master suite with a vaulted ceiling and access to the veranda reside in the right wing. Two additional bedrooms with two baths and a loft overlooking the gathering room are upstairs. A large bonus room is found over the garage and can be developed later as office or hobby space.

plan #

HPT9800027

STYLE: FRENCH COUNTRY
FIRST FLOOR: 2,390 SQ. FT.
SECOND FLOOR: 765 SQ. FT.
TOTAL: 3,155 SQ. FT.
BONUS SPACE: 433 SQ. FT.
BEDROOMS: 4
BATHROOMS: 3½
WIDTH: 87' - 11"
DEPTH: 75' - 2"
FOUNDATION: CRAWLSPACE

SEARCH ONLINE @ EPLANS.COM

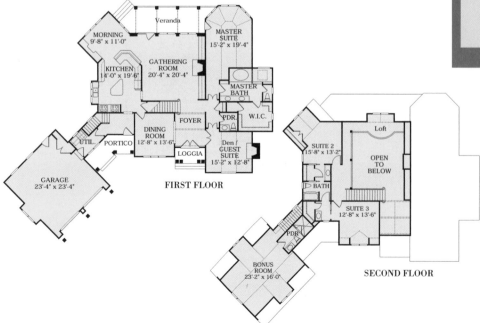

REAR EXTERIOR

plan
HPT9800138

STYLE: COUNTRY COTTAGE

FIRST FLOOR: 2,438 SQ. FT.

SECOND FLOOR: 882 SQ. FT.

TOTAL: 3,320 SQ. FT.

BONUS SPACE: 230 SQ. FT.

BEDROOMS: 4

BATHROOMS: 4½

WIDTH: 70' - 0"

DEPTH: 63' - 2"

FOUNDATION: Basement, Slab

SEARCH ONLINE @ EPLANS.COM

Wonderful rooflines top a brick exterior with cedar-and-stone accents and lots of English Country charm. The two-story entry reveals a graceful curving staircase and opens to the formal living and dining rooms. Fireplaces are found in the living room as well as the great room, which also boasts built-in bookcases and access to the rear patio. The kitchen and breakfast room add to the informal area and include a snack bar. A private patio is part of the master suite, which also offers a lavish bath, a large walk-in closet, and a nearby study. Three family bedrooms and a bonus room complete the second floor.

SECOND FLOOR

FIRST FLOOR

plan #

HPT9800139

STYLE: FRENCH
SQUARE FOOTAGE: 3,230
BEDROOMS: 3
BATHROOMS: 3
WIDTH: 94' - 8"
DEPTH: 88' - 5"
FOUNDATION: SLAB

SEARCH ONLINE @ EPLANS.COM

A mini-estate with French Country details, this home preserves the beauty of historical design without sacrificing modern convenience. Through double doors, the floor plan opens from a central foyer flanked by a dining room and a study. The family room offers windows overlooking the rear yard and a fireplace. The master bedroom suite features a sitting room and bath fit for royalty. A smaller family bedroom has a full bath nearby. A third bedroom also enjoys a full bath.

plan #

HPT9800140

STYLE: EUROPEAN COTTAGE
FIRST FLOOR: 2,655 SQ. FT.
SECOND FLOOR: 820 SQ. FT.
TOTAL: 3,475 SQ. FT.
BEDROOMS: 4
BATHROOMS: 4½
WIDTH: 74' - 0"
DEPTH: 78' - 0"
FOUNDATION: SLAB

SEARCH ONLINE @ EPLANS.COM

French opulence is the theme of this classical
European cottage. Symmetry, stucco, and French shutters dazzle the exterior. Stately columns frame the
front porch. The foyer is flanked on either side by a
study with a fireplace and a formal living room with
another fireplace. Straight ahead, a sunroom views the
rear porch. The kitchen is set between the formal
dining room and the casual eating area. A two-car
garage with abundant storage is located nearby. On the
opposite side of the home, the master suite features a
private bath with a bayed tub and His and Hers walk-
in closets. The guest bedroom with a walk-in closet is
placed next to a full hall bath. A utility room is located
nearby. Upstairs, two additional bedrooms offer sitting
areas, private baths, walk-in closets, and built-ins.

SECOND FLOOR

FIRST FLOOR

Unusual chimneys, varied rooflines, and European window treatments enhance the stone-and-stucco exterior of this breathtaking home. Inside, is the great room, featuring a fireplace flanked by bookcases, a snack bar, and two doors to the rear terrace. A semicircle of windows outlines the breakfast nook, which opens off the kitchen, a wonderful work area with a cooktop island, a walk-in pantry, and ample counter space. The formal dining room is a few steps from both the kitchen and the front door, making entertaining easy. To the left of the foyer, a study with a beam ceiling and a second fireplace serves as a quiet retreat. The first-floor master suite is sure to please with a sunny sitting area, a large walk-in closet, and a pampering bath. A second-floor balcony connects three family bedrooms, two baths, and a bonus room.

plan #

HPT9800037

STYLE: COUNTRY COTTAGE
FIRST FLOOR: 2,145 SQ. FT.
SECOND FLOOR: 1,310 SQ. FT.
TOTAL: 3,455 SQ. FT.
BONUS SPACE: 308 SQ. FT.
BEDROOMS: 4
BATHROOMS: 3½
WIDTH: 67' - 0"
DEPTH: 59' - 4"
FOUNDATION: CRAWLSPACE

SEARCH ONLINE @ EPLANS.COM

Ideal Golf Course Home

FIRST FLOOR

TERRACE
SITTING 12'-4" x 10'-0"
BREAKFAST 12'-4" x 10'-0"
W.I.C.
MASTER SUITE 14'-4" x 12'-6"
GREAT ROOM 19'-0" x 16'-0"
KITCHEN 16'-0" x 12'-0"
P.
MASTER BATH
LAUNDRY
PDR.
FOYER
DINING ROOM 12'-8" x 13'-6"
GARAGE 22'-10" x 22'-0"
STUDY 14'-4" x 12'-6"
PORTICO

SECOND FLOOR

OPEN TO BELOW
SUITE 4 14'-4" x 13'-8"
SUITE 3 14'-4" x 13'-0"
BATH
W.I.C.
BALCONY
BATH
OPEN TO BELOW
SUITE 2 12'-8" x 13'-6"
BONUS 12'-0" x 20'-0"

plan #

HPT9800141

STYLE: EUROPEAN COTTAGE
FIRST FLOOR: 2,219 SQ. FT.
SECOND FLOOR: 1,085 SQ. FT.
TOTAL: 3,304 SQ. FT.
BONUS SPACE: 404 SQ. FT.
BEDROOMS: 4
BATHROOMS: 3½
WIDTH: 91' - 0"
DEPTH: 52' - 8"
FOUNDATION: SLAB

SEARCH ONLINE @ EPLANS.COM

This home features two levels of pampering luxury filled with the most up-to-date amenities. Touches of Mediterranean detail add to the striking facade. A wrapping front porch welcomes you inside to a formal dining room and two-story great room warmed by a fireplace. Double doors from the master suite, great room, and breakfast nook access the rear veranda. The first-floor master suite enjoys a luxury bath, roomy walk-in closet, and close access to the front-facing office/study. Three additional bedrooms reside upstairs. The bonus room above the garage is great for an apartment or storage space.

SECOND FLOOR

FIRST FLOOR

© 2002 Donald A. Gardner, Inc.

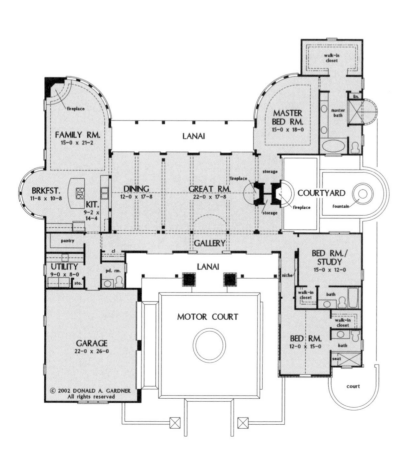

© 2002 Donald A. Gardner
All rights reserved

plan #

HPT9800142

STYLE: RANCH

SQUARE FOOTAGE: 3,061

BEDROOMS: 3

BATHROOMS: 3½

WIDTH: 86' - 1"

DEPTH: 84' - 8"

SEARCH ONLINE @ EPLANS.COM

This updated hacienda offers the utmost in livability. Enter through a rugged stone lanai to an elegant gallery hall, which accesses the combined great room/dining area. A double-sided fireplace warms this space as well as the courtyard to the right. The adjacent master suite features a curved wall of windows and a deluxe bath with a huge walk-in closet. On the opposite side of the plan, the kitchen's serving-bar island looks into the bay-windowed breakfast nook. A roomy pantry will delight the family cook. A utility room and half-bath are convenient to both the kitchen and the two-car garage. Opening from the other side of the kitchen is a hearth-warmed family room that accesses the rear lanai. At the right front of the plan reside two additional bedrooms—each with its own bath.

plan
HPT9800143

STYLE: FLORIDIAN
FIRST FLOOR: 2,853 SQ. FT.
SECOND FLOOR: 627 SQ. FT.
TOTAL: 3,480 SQ. FT.
GUEST HOUSE: 312 SQ. FT.
BEDROOMS: 3
BATHROOMS: 2½
WIDTH: 80' - 0"
DEPTH: 96' - 0"
FOUNDATION: SLAB

L

SEARCH ONLINE @ EPLANS.COM

A unique courtyard provides a happy medium for indoor/outdoor living in this design. Inside, the foyer opens to a grand salon with a wall of glass, providing unobstructed views of the backyard. Informal areas include a leisure room with an entertainment center and glass doors that open to a covered poolside lanai. An outdoor fireplace enhances casual gatherings. The master suite is filled with amenities that include a bayed sitting area, access to the rear lanai, His and Hers closets, and a soaking tub. Upstairs, two family bedrooms—both with private decks—share a full bath. A detached guest house has a cabana bath and an outdoor grill area.

SECOND FLOOR

Perfect Waterfront Plan

FIRST FLOOR

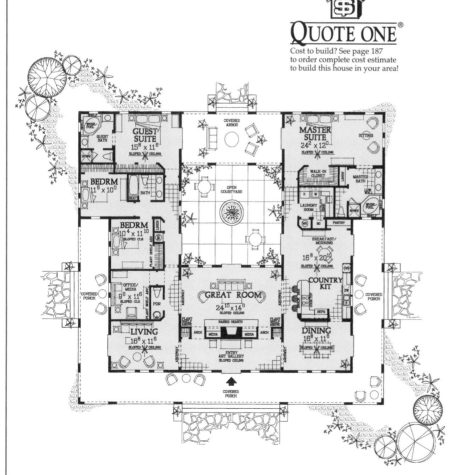

Quote One®

Cost to build? See page 187
to order complete cost estimate
to build this house in your area!

ptan#

HPT9800144

STYLE: MEDITERRANEAN

SQUARE FOOTAGE: 3,163

BEDROOMS: 4

BATHROOMS: 3½

WIDTH: 75' - 2"

DEPTH: 68' - 8"

FOUNDATION: SLAB

L

SEARCH ONLINE @ EPLANS.COM

An open courtyard takes center stage in this home, providing a happy marriage of indoor/outdoor relationships. Art collectors will appreciate the gallery that enhances the entry and showcases their favorite works. The centrally located great room supplies the nucleus for formal and informal entertaining. A raised-hearth fireplace flanked by built-in media centers adds a special touch. The master suite provides a private retreat where you may relax—try the sitting room or retire to the private bath for a pampering soak in the corner whirlpool tub.

plan #

HPT9800008

STYLE: MEDITERRANEAN

SQUARE FOOTAGE: 3,424

BONUS SPACE: 507 SQ. FT.

BEDROOMS: 5

BATHROOMS: 4

WIDTH: 82' - 4"

DEPTH: 83' - 8"

FOUNDATION: SLAB

SEARCH ONLINE @ EPLANS.COM

This lovely five-bedroom home exudes the beauty and warmth of a Mediterranean villa. The foyer views explode in all directions with the dominant use of octagonal shapes throughout. Double doors lead to the master wing, which abounds with niches. The sitting area of the master bedroom has a commanding view of the rear gardens. A bedroom just off the master suite is perfect for a guest room or office. The formal living and dining rooms share expansive glass walls and marble or tile pathways. The mitered glass wall of the breakfast nook can be viewed from the huge island kitchen. Two secondary bedrooms share the convenience of a Pullman-style bath. An additional rear bedroom completes this design.

Honored traditions are echoed throughout this warm and inviting Santa Fe home. A large, two-story gathering room with a beehive fireplace provides a soothing atmosphere for entertaining or quiet interludes. A gallery leads to the kitchen and breakfast area where abundant counter space and a work island will please the fussiest of cooks. A nearby laundry room provides entry to the three-car garage. On the right side of the plan, the master suite offers a private study, a fireplace, and a luxurious bath with dual lavatories, a whirlpool tub, and a curved shower. On the second floor, a reading loft with built-in bookshelves complements three family bedrooms.

plan#
HPT9800145
STYLE: SW CONTEMPORARY
FIRST FLOOR: 2,401 SQ. FT.
SECOND FLOOR: 927 SQ. FT.
TOTAL: 3,328 SQ. FT.
BEDROOMS: 4
BATHROOMS: 3
WIDTH: 104' - 9"
DEPTH: 62' - 5"
FOUNDATION: SLAB

SEARCH ONLINE @ EPLANS.COM

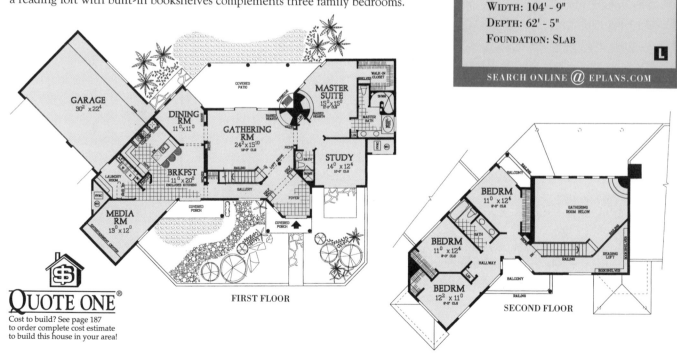

FIRST FLOOR

SECOND FLOOR

Quote One®
Cost to build? See page 187 to order complete cost estimate to build this house in your area!

plan #

HPT9800146

STYLE: TRADITIONAL
FIRST FLOOR: 2,813 SQ. FT.
SECOND FLOOR: 1,091 SQ. FT.
TOTAL: 3,904 SQ. FT.
BEDROOMS: 4
BATHROOMS: 3½
WIDTH: 85' - 5"
DEPTH: 74' - 8"

SEARCH ONLINE @ EPLANS.COM

Keystone lintels and an arched transom over the entry spell classic design for this four-bedroom home. The tiled foyer offers entry to any room you choose, whether it's the secluded den with its built-in bookshelves, the formal dining room, the formal living room with its fireplace, or the spacious rear family room and kitchen area with a sunny breakfast nook. The first-floor master suite features a sitting room with bookshelves, two walk-in closets, and a private bath with a corner whirlpool tub. Upstairs, two family bedrooms share a bath and enjoy separate vanities. A third family bedroom features its own full bath and a built-in window seat in a box-bay window.

SECOND FLOOR

FIRST FLOOR

REAR EXTERIOR

Although the exterior of this Georgian home is entirely classical, the interior boasts an up-to-date floor plan that's a perfect fit for today's lifestyles. The large central family room, conveniently near the kitchen and breakfast area, includes a fireplace and access to the rear terrace; fireplaces also grace the formal dining room and library. The master suite, also with terrace access, features a spacious walk-in closet and a bath with a whirlpool tub. Upstairs, a second master suite—great for guests—joins two family bedrooms. Nearby, a large open area can serve as a recreation room.

plan #

HPT9800147

STYLE: COLONIAL
FIRST FLOOR: 2,492 SQ. FT.
SECOND FLOOR: 1,313 SQ. FT.
TOTAL: 3,805 SQ. FT.
BONUS SPACE: 687 SQ. FT.
BEDROOMS: 4
BATHROOMS: 3½ + ½
WIDTH: 85' - 10"
DEPTH: 54' - 6"
FOUNDATION: BASEMENT, CRAWLSPACE

SEARCH ONLINE @ EPLANS.COM

FIRST FLOOR

SECOND FLOOR

ptan#

HPT9800148

STYLE: TRADITIONAL
FIRST FLOOR: 2,306 SQ. FT.
SECOND FLOOR: 1,544 SQ. FT.
TOTAL: 3,850 SQ. FT.
BEDROOMS: 5
BATHROOMS: 3½
WIDTH: 80' - 8"
DEPTH: 51' - 8"
FOUNDATION: BASEMENT

SEARCH ONLINE @ EPLANS.COM

The detailed keystone arch highlights the grand entryway of this home. The vast windows flood the home with natural light throughout. The entry leads into a splendid great room with a sunken solarium. The solarium features U-shaped stairs and a balcony with an arched window. The secluded master suite includes a luxurious bath and a large study with a bay window. A loft, the library, and four family bedrooms occupy the second floor.

SECOND FLOOR

FIRST FLOOR

European accents shape the exterior of this striking family home. Inside, the foyer is open to the dining room on the right and the living room straight ahead. Here, two sets of double doors open to the rear covered porch. Casual areas of the home include a family room warmed by a fireplace and an island kitchen opening to a bayed breakfast room. The first-floor master retreat is a luxurious perk, which offers a bayed sitting area, a whirlpool bath, and large His and Hers walk-in closets. Bedroom 2—with its close proximity to the master suite—is perfect for a nursery or home office. Upstairs, Bedrooms 3 and 4 boast walk-in closets and share a bath. Future space is available off the game room.

plan #

HPT9800149

STYLE: EUROPEAN COTTAGE
FIRST FLOOR: 2,654 SQ. FT.
SECOND FLOOR: 1,013 SQ. FT.
TOTAL: 3,667 SQ. FT.
BONUS SPACE: 192 SQ. FT.
BEDROOMS: 4
BATHROOMS: 3½
WIDTH: 75' - 4"
DEPTH: 74' - 2"
FOUNDATION: CRAWLSPACE,
BASEMENT, SLAB

SEARCH ONLINE @ EPLANS.COM

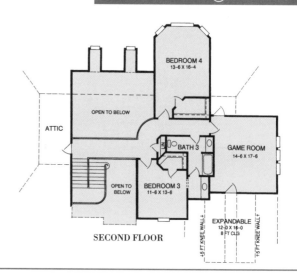

FIRST FLOOR

SECOND FLOOR

plan#
HPT9800150

STYLE: CONTEMPORARY
FIRST FLOOR: 1,550 SQ. FT.
SECOND FLOOR: 2,102 SQ. FT.
TOTAL: 3,652 SQ. FT.
BEDROOMS: 4
BATHROOMS: 3½
WIDTH: 60' - 3"
DEPTH: 65' - 5"

SEARCH ONLINE @ EPLANS.COM

This sleek, contemporary design features an octagonal gameroom and a corner master bedroom with angled master bath and sundeck access. The island kitchen, breakfast area with porch access, and family room share a large living area to the rear of the home—ideal for casual gatherings. A parlor rounds out the main floor. Upstairs, three secondary bedrooms are outfitted with walk-in closets and full bath access. A game room facilitates family activities and provides a buffer between family rooms and the master suite.

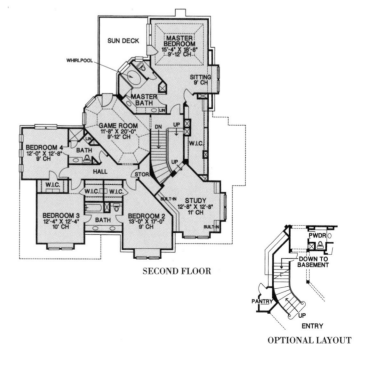

SECOND FLOOR

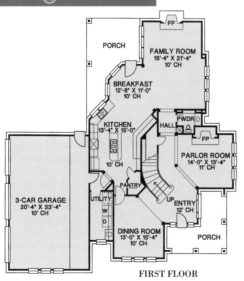

FIRST FLOOR

OPTIONAL LAYOUT

Anyone walking through this home will be dazzled by the walls of windows and delighted by the bayed dining room, study, gameroom, and two secondary bedrooms. The great room offers a wonderful view from its triple windows and rear-porch access. The kitchen sports an island work station and bright breakfast room. The dining room is elegant with a bay window. The first-floor master suite offers privacy and luxury with a full bath, walk-in closets, and whirlpool tub.

plan #

HPT9800151

STYLE: EUROPEAN COTTAGE
FIRST FLOOR: 2,200 SQ. FT.
SECOND FLOOR: 1,338 SQ. FT.
TOTAL: 3,538 SQ. FT.
BEDROOMS: 4
BATHROOMS: 3½
WIDTH: 83' - 5"
DEPTH: 68' - 11"

SEARCH ONLINE @ EPLANS.COM

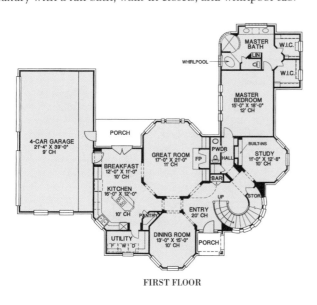

FIRST FLOOR

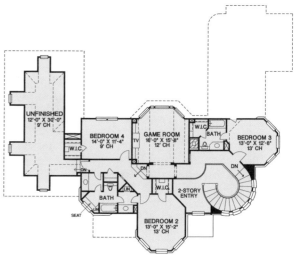

SECOND FLOOR

plan #

HPT9800152

STYLE: CONTEMPORARY
FIRST FLOOR: 3,370 SQ. FT.
SECOND FLOOR: 514 SQ. FT.
TOTAL: 3,884 SQ. FT.
BEDROOMS: 4
BATHROOMS: 3½
WIDTH: 97' - 0"
DEPTH: 79' - 0"

SEARCH ONLINE @ EPLANS.COM

Newlyweds will love this home, which offers His-and-Hers space throughout—including separate baths and walk-in closets in the master suite. There's plenty of room for get togethers in the island kitchen, breakfast nook, and the great room. Family and friends will be comfortably entertained in the formal dining room. A spacious den connecting to a study offers a quiet retreat.

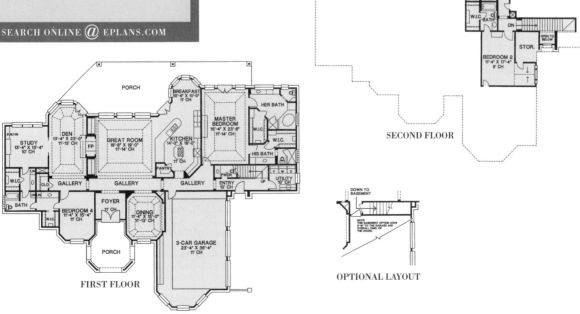

SECOND FLOOR

FIRST FLOOR

OPTIONAL LAYOUT

Columns and arches distinguish the front porch of this attractive, shingle-sided home. The foyer includes a convenient powder room for guests. Two sets of French doors lead to the deck or terrace from the gathering room, which has a cozy fireplace. The efficient kitchen will easily serve a quiet dinner in the adjacent breakfast nook, or a grand banquet in the nearby dining room. The master suite is located near the vaulted study, and enjoys a bayed window and amenity-filled bath. Three upper-level bedrooms share a central gathering area and access to a large bonus room.

plan #

HPT9800005

STYLE: COUNTRY COTTAGE
FIRST FLOOR: 2,202 SQ. FT.
SECOND FLOOR: 1,355 SQ. FT.
TOTAL: 3,557 SQ. FT.
BONUS SPACE: 523 SQ. FT.
BEDROOMS: 4
BATHROOMS: 3½
WIDTH: 66' - 0"
DEPTH: 65' - 10"
FOUNDATION: CRAWLSPACE

SEARCH ONLINE @ EPLANS.COM

plan #

HPT9800013

STYLE: COUNTRY COTTAGE
FIRST FLOOR: 2,436 SQ. FT.
SECOND FLOOR: 1,401 SQ. FT.
TOTAL: 3,837 SQ. FT.
BONUS SPACE: 330 SQ. FT.
BEDROOMS: 3
BATHROOMS: 3½
WIDTH: 107' - 0"
DEPTH: 60' - 0"
FOUNDATION: CRAWLSPACE

SEARCH ONLINE @ EPLANS.COM

A beautiful arched entry begins the country charm of this plantation cottage. Continue inside to a welcoming foyer with a living room on the left and dining room on the right. The grand room is aptly named and serves as a comfortable receiving area. At the rear, the gathering room is a casual place to relax in front of a warming fire. Situated for privacy, the master suite excels with a unique room shape, patio access, dual walk-in closets, and a soothing bath designed for two. Upstairs, dormer windows light every room, including the bonus space over the garage.

With a gazebo-style covered porch and careful exterior details, you can't help but imagine tea parties, porch swings, and lazy summer evenings. Inside, a living room/library will comfort with its fireplace and built-ins. The family room is graced with a fireplace and a curved, two-story ceiling with an overlook above. The master bedroom is a private retreat with a lovely bath, twin walk-in closets, and rear-porch access. Upstairs, three bedrooms with sizable closets—one bedroom would make an excellent guest suite or alternate master suite—share access to expandable space.

plan #

HPT9800153

STYLE: FARMHOUSE
FIRST FLOOR: 2,442 SQ. FT.
SECOND FLOOR: 1,286 SQ. FT.
TOTAL: 3,728 SQ. FT.
BONUS SPACE: 681 SQ. FT.
BEDROOMS: 4
BATHROOMS: 3½ + ½
WIDTH: 84' - 8"
DEPTH: 60' - 0"
FOUNDATION: CRAWLSPACE

SEARCH ONLINE @ EPLANS.COM

FIRST FLOOR

SECOND FLOOR

plan
HPT9800154

STYLE: COUNTRY COTTAGE
FIRST FLOOR: 2,225 SQ. FT.
SECOND FLOOR: 1,360 SQ. FT.
TOTAL: 3,585 SQ. FT.
BONUS SPACE: 277 SQ. FT.
BEDROOMS: 4
BATHROOMS: 3½
WIDTH: 68' - 10"
DEPTH: 60' - 0"
FOUNDATION: BASEMENT, CRAWLSPACE

SEARCH ONLINE @ EPLANS.COM

This breathtaking stone-and-shingle European cottage will turn the home of your dreams into a reality. Enter to a formal foyer with an elegant box-bay dining room on the left and vast vaulted family room ahead. A fireplace here gives the room a definite focus; tall windows bring in floods of natural light. An expansive kitchen makes it easy for multiple cooks to share space and effortlessly serve the bayed breakfast nook. A vaulted keeping room at the rear is a cozy hideaway. The master suite shines with a bayed sitting area and majestic vaulted bath with a corner garden tub.

SECOND FLOOR

FIRST FLOOR

A symmetrical facade with twin chimneys makes a grand statement. A covered porch welcomes visitors and provides a pleasant place to spend a mild evening. The foyer is flanked by formal living areas—a dining room and a living room—each with a fireplace. A third fireplace is the highlight of the expansive great room to the rear. An L-shaped kitchen offers a work island and a walk-in pantry and easily serves the nearby breakfast and sunrooms. The master suite provides lavish luxuries.

plan #

HPT9800155

STYLE: TRADITIONAL
FIRST FLOOR: 2,565 SQ. FT.
SECOND FLOOR: 1,375 SQ. FT.
TOTAL: 3,940 SQ. FT.
BEDROOMS: 4
BATHROOMS: 3½
WIDTH: 88' - 6"
DEPTH: 58' - 6"
FOUNDATION: WALKOUT BASEMENT

SEARCH ONLINE @ EPLANS.COM

FIRST FLOOR

REAR EXTERIOR

SECOND FLOOR

plan #

HPT9800156

STYLE: NORMAN
FIRST FLOOR: 2,729 SQ. FT.
SECOND FLOOR: 1,157 SQ. FT.
TOTAL: 3,886 SQ. FT.
BEDROOMS: 4
BATHROOMS: 3½
WIDTH: 73' - 11"
DEPTH: 70' - 11"
FOUNDATION: BASEMENT

SEARCH ONLINE @ EPLANS.COM

A stately facade joins with an elegant interior floor plan to bring luxury and casual space together creating an exceptional home. A private study just off the foyer is ideal as a home office or after-dinner relaxation spot. The formal dining room is open to the great room, featuring a large bow window. The kitchen is the perfect hub of family activities with an island, breakfast area, and adjoining family room with fireplace. Secluded and comfortable, the master suite provides a cozy sitting area with a fireplace, a spacious bath with oversize walk-in closet, and comparmented toilet. Upstairs three family bedrooms, a loft, and two full baths complete this plan.

SECOND FLOOR

FIRST FLOOR

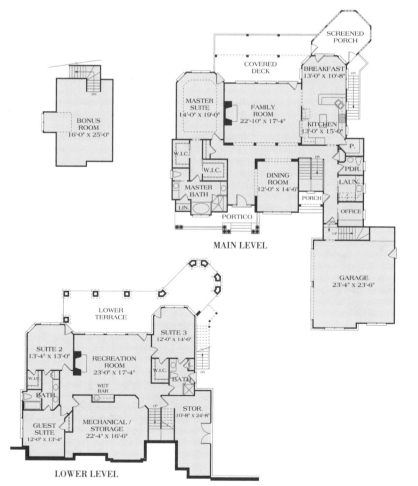

BONUS
ROOM
16'-0" x 25'-0"

SCREENED
PORCH

COVERED
DECK

BREAKFAST
13'-0" x 10'-8"

MASTER
SUITE
14'-0" x 19'-0"

FAMILY
ROOM
22'-10" x 17'-4"

KITCHEN
13'-0" x 15'-0"

W.I.C.

W.I.C.

P.

DINING
ROOM
12'-0" x 14'-6"

PDR.

LAUN.

MASTER
BATH

LIN.

PORCH

OFFICE

PORTICO

MAIN LEVEL

LOWER
TERRACE

SUITE 3
12'-0" x 14'-6"

SUITE 2
13'-4" x 13'-0"

RECREATION
ROOM
23'-0" x 17'-4"

W.I.C.

W.I.C.

BATH

BATH

WET
BAR

GUEST
SUITE
12'-0" x 13'-4"

MECHANICAL /
STORAGE
22'-4" x 16'-6"

STOR.
10'-8" x 24'-8"

GARAGE
23'-4" x 23'-6"

LOWER LEVEL

plan

HPT9800157

STYLE: COUNTRY COTTAGE
MAIN LEVEL: 2,213 SQ. FT.
LOWER LEVEL: 1,333 SQ. FT.
TOTAL: 3,546 SQ. FT.
BONUS SPACE: 430 SQ. FT.
BEDROOMS: 4
BATHROOMS: 3½
WIDTH: 67' - 2"
DEPTH: 93' - 1"
FOUNDATION: BASEMENT

SEARCH ONLINE @ EPLANS.COM

Interesting window treatments highlight this stone-and-shake facade, but don't overlook the columned porch to the left of the portico. Arches outline the formal dining room and the family room, both of which are convenient to the island kitchen. Household chores are made easier by the placement of a pantry, powder room, laundry room, and office between the kitchen and the entrances to the side porch and garage. If your goal is relaxation, the breakfast room, screened porch, and covered deck are also nearby. The master suite features a beautiful bay, and three secondary bedrooms and a recreation room are on the lower level.

ptan #

HPT9800158

STYLE: COUNTRY COTTAGE
FIRST FLOOR: 2,660 SQ. FT.
SECOND FLOOR: 914 SQ. FT.
TOTAL: 3,574 SQ. FT.
BONUS SPACE: 733 SQ. FT.
BEDROOMS: 3
BATHROOMS: 4½
WIDTH: 114' - 8"
DEPTH: 75' - 10"
FOUNDATION: CRAWLSPACE

SEARCH ONLINE @ EPLANS.COM

Gently curved arches and dormers contrast with the straight lines of gables and wooden columns on this French-style stone exterior. Small-paned windows are enhanced by shutters; tall chimneys and a cupola add height. Inside, a spacious gathering room with an impressive fireplace opens to a cheery morning room. The kitchen is a delight, with a beam ceiling, triangular work island, walk-in pantry, and angular counter with a snack bar. The nearby laundry room includes a sink, a work area, and plenty of room for storage. The first-floor master suite boasts a bay-windowed sitting nook, a deluxe bath, and a handy study.

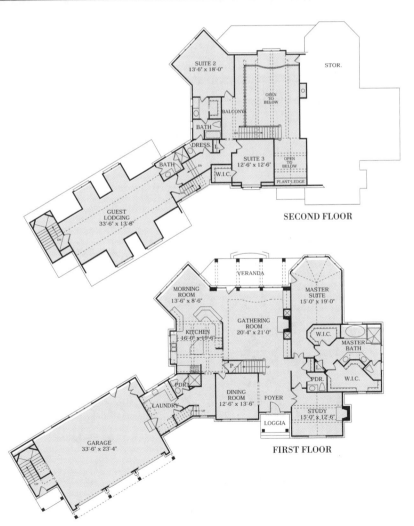

SECOND FLOOR

FIRST FLOOR

© The Sater Group, Inc.

Ensure an elegant lifestyle with this luxurious plan. A turret, two-story bay windows, and plenty of arched glass impart a graceful style to the exterior, and rich amenities inside furnish contentment. A grand foyer decked with columns introduces the living room with curved-glass windows viewing the rear gardens. The study and living room share a through-fireplace. The master suite enjoys a tray ceiling, two walk-in closets, a separate shower, and a garden tub set in a bay window. Informal entertainment will be a breeze with a rich leisure room adjoining the kitchen and breakfast nook and opening to a rear veranda. Upstairs, two family bedrooms and a guest suite with a private deck complete the plan.

plan #

HPT9800159

STYLE: ITALIANATE
FIRST FLOOR: 2,841 SQ. FT.
SECOND FLOOR: 1,052 SQ. FT.
TOTAL: 3,893 SQ. FT.
BEDROOMS: 4
BATHROOMS: 3½
WIDTH: 85' - 0"
DEPTH: 76' - 8"
FOUNDATION: BASEMENT, SLAB

SEARCH ONLINE @ EPLANS.COM

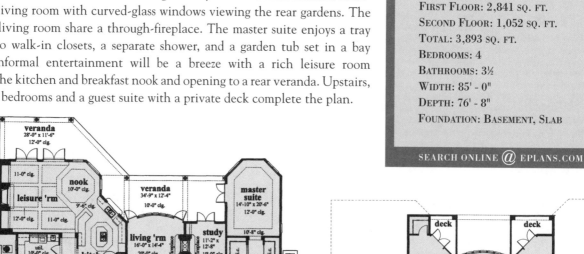

FIRST FLOOR

SECOND FLOOR

plan
HPT9800160

STYLE: ITALIANATE
FIRST FLOOR: 2,391 SQ. FT.
SECOND FLOOR: 1,539 SQ. FT.
TOTAL: 3,930 SQ. FT.
BEDROOMS: 3
BATHROOMS: 3½
WIDTH: 71' - 0"
DEPTH: 69' - 0"
FOUNDATION: BASEMENT

SEARCH ONLINE @ EPLANS.COM

Impressive pillars, keystone lintel arches, a covered carport, an abundance of windows, and an alluring fountain are just a few of the decorative touches of this elegant design. The two-story foyer leads to a two-story great room, which enjoys built-in cabinetry, a two-sided fireplace, and spectacular views to the rear property. To the left of the great room is the dining area, with a wet bar, island kitchen, and nearby bayed breakfast nook. Bedroom 2 boasts a semicircular wall of windows, a full bath, and a walk-in closet. The second-floor master suite is filled with amenities, including a two-sided fireplace.

SECOND FLOOR

FIRST FLOOR

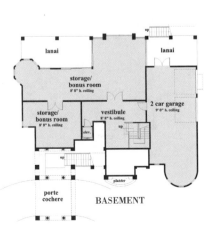

BASEMENT

Chic and glamorous, this Mediterranean facade pairs ancient shapes, such as square columns, with a refined disposition set off by radius windows. A magnificent entry leads to an interior gallery and the great room. This extraordinary space is warmed by a two-sided fireplace and defined by extended views of the rear property. The gourmet kitchen easily serves any occasion and provides a pass-through to the outdoor kitchen. Double doors open to the master suite, which features a walk-in closet, two-sided fireplace and angled whirlpool bath. The upper-level catwalk leads to a bedroom suite that can easily accommodate a guest or live-in relative.

plan #

HPT9800161

STYLE: ITALIANATE
FIRST FLOOR: 2,491 SQ. FT.
SECOND FLOOR: 1,290 SQ. FT.
TOTAL: 3,781 SQ. FT.
BEDROOMS: 5
BATHROOMS: 4½
WIDTH: 62' - 0"
DEPTH: 67' - 0"
FOUNDATION: BASEMENT

SEARCH ONLINE @ EPLANS.COM

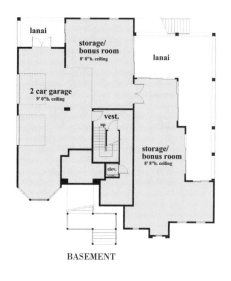

BASEMENT

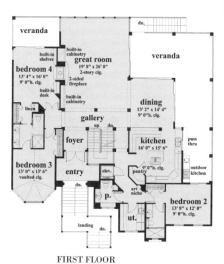

FIRST FLOOR

SECOND FLOOR

plan

HPT9800012

STYLE: MEDITERRANEAN
FIRST FLOOR: 1,900 SQ. FT.
SECOND FLOOR: 1,676 SQ. FT.
TOTAL: 3,576 SQ. FT.
BEDROOMS: 3
BATHROOMS: 3½
WIDTH: 67' - 0"
DEPTH: 82' - 6"
FOUNDATION: CRAWLSPACE

SEARCH ONLINE @ EPLANS.COM

Absolutely gorgeous from any angle, this Mediterranean villa will delight and inspire. Enter off the front terrace to the formal foyer; the living room (or study) opens on the right through French doors. The nearby dining room is graced with French doors that lead out to the terrace and bring fresh air in. Abundant counter space in the kitchen makes it simple to serve the adjoining breakfast nook. The great room hosts an enchanting beamed ceiling, large, warming fireplace, and access to the rear terrace. Upstairs, two bedrooms, each with its own bath, share a sitting area and lovely balcony. A lavish bath and wrapping balcony mark the master suite and make this retreat as a true haven.

SECOND FLOOR

FIRST FLOOR

Mediterranean accents enhance the facade of this contemporary estate home. Two fanciful turret bays add a sense of grandeur to the exterior. Double doors open inside to a grand two-story foyer. A two-sided fireplace warms the study and living room, with a two-story coffered ceiling. To the right, the master suite includes a private bath, two walk-in closets, and double-door access to the sweeping rear veranda. Casual areas of the home include the gourmet island kitchen, breakfast nook, and leisure room warmed by a fireplace. A spiral staircase leads upstairs, where a second-floor balcony separates two family bedrooms from the luxurious guest suite.

plan #

HPT9800162

STYLE: EUROPEAN COTTAGE
FIRST FLOOR: 2,834 SQ. FT.
SECOND FLOOR: 1,143 SQ. FT.
TOTAL: 3,977 SQ. FT.
BEDROOMS: 4
BATHROOMS: 3½
WIDTH: 85' - 0"
DEPTH: 76' - 8"
FOUNDATION: SLAB

SEARCH ONLINE @ EPLANS.COM

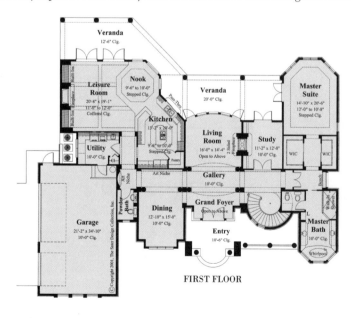

FIRST FLOOR

SECOND FLOOR

plan
HPT9800025

STYLE: TRADITIONAL
MAIN LEVEL: 2,792 SQ. FT.
LOWER LEVEL: 2,016 SQ. FT.
TOTAL: 4,808 SQ. FT.
BEDROOMS: 4
BATHROOMS: 4½
WIDTH: 81' - 0"
DEPTH: 66' - 0"
FOUNDATION: BASEMENT

SEARCH ONLINE @ EPLANS.COM

This grand manor boasts an open interior packed with fabulous amenities. The spacious foyer opens to the formal dining room, which leads to a well-organized gourmet kitchen through a butler's pantry. Mitered glass allows wide views in the dining room, while French doors open the great room to a wraparound deck. A corner fireplace warms the living space and shares its glow with the central interior. Double doors lead to a secluded den—a room so convenient to the foyer that it would easily convert to a home office. To the rear of the plan, a rambling master suite offers its own access to the rear deck.

REAR EXTERIOR

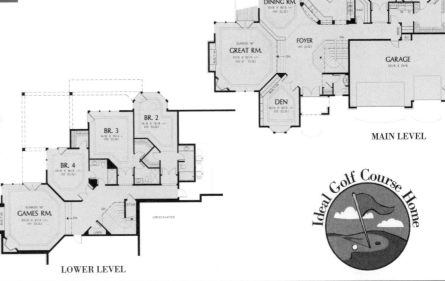

MAIN LEVEL

LOWER LEVEL

With contemporary styling, this seaside vacation home offers great livability and outdoor spaces. The foyer, solarium, living room, family room, and media room all boast vaulted ceilings. The sunken living room shares a through-fireplace with the formal dining room, which has access to an outdoor area. Skylights illuminate the foyer, solarium, gallery, and bathrooms. The sunken master suite enjoys a private deck and a spiral staircase to the loft. The media room is graced by a wet bar, audiovisual center, clerestory windows, and a deck overlooking the solarium. Each secondary bedroom includes a private vanity; Bedroom 2 has a built-in desk.

plan #

HPT9800163

STYLE: NW CONTEMPORARY
FIRST FLOOR: 2,690 SQ. FT.
SECOND FLOOR: 1,406 SQ. FT.
TOTAL: 4,096 SQ. FT.
BEDROOMS: 3
BATHROOMS: 2½
WIDTH: 65' - 4"
DEPTH: 67' - 0"
FOUNDATION: BASEMENT, CRAWLSPACE

SEARCH ONLINE @ EPLANS.COM

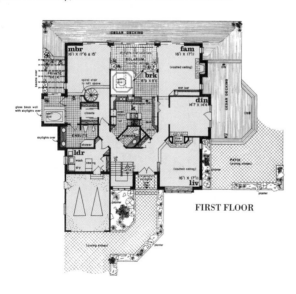

FIRST FLOOR

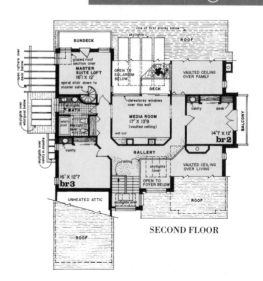

SECOND FLOOR

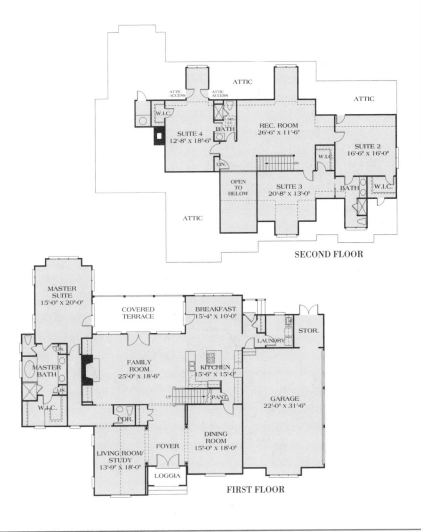

ptan #

HPT9800164

STYLE: CRAFTSMAN
FIRST FLOOR: 3,562 SQ. FT.
SECOND FLOOR: 1,594 SQ. FT.
TOTAL: 5,156 SQ. FT.
BASEMENT: 2,346 SQ. FT.
BEDROOMS: 4
BATHROOMS: 4½
WIDTH: 74' - 6"
DEPTH: 92' - 0"
FOUNDATION: BASEMENT

SEARCH ONLINE @ EPLANS.COM

Exquisite Craftsman character is the hallmark of this incredible design. A front loggia welcomes you inside to a foyer where the curved staircase is flanked by a dining room and a study. The gathering room is warmed by a fireplace flanked by built-ins. The master suite is enhanced with a spacious sitting area, pampering whirlpool bath, and large walk-in closet. The gourmet kitchen extends into a morning nook that accesses the rear covered terrace. Three additional suites are located upstairs, along with a spacious study loft. Don't miss the impressive basement level, which includes a recreation room served by a bar, an entertainment room with a fireplace, and access to the covered terrace, an exercise room, and a handy workshop area.

A modern interpretation of a classic ranch estate, this house plan's exterior features stately columns, decorative wood brackets, and an inviting front porch. Rugged stonework combines with gentle arches in the front clerestory, dormer windows, and entryway to add architectural interest. Inside, decorative ceilings with exposed wood beams top the master bedroom, great room, dining room, and screened porch. This hillside home boasts four fireplaces and a rear wall of windows that capture exceptional views. Other custom-styled elements include a wet bar in the media room and a private study/sitting area in the master suite. Lush yet practical, this home provides an abundance of storage and counter space as seen in the kitchen and laundry/ mudroom.

plan #

HPT9800165

STYLE: TRADITIONAL
MAIN LEVEL: 3,040 SQ. FT.
LOWER LEVEL: 1,736 SQ. FT.
TOTAL: 4,776 SQ. FT.
BEDROOMS: 5
BATHROOMS: 4½ + ½
WIDTH: 106' - 1"
DEPTH: 104' - 2"

SEARCH ONLINE @ EPLANS.COM

LOWER LEVEL

MAIN LEVEL

Great for a Mountainside Lot

plan #

HPT9800166

STYLE: CRAFTSMAN
MAIN LEVEL: 3,040 SQ. FT.
LOWER LEVEL: 1,736 SQ. FT.
TOTAL: 4,776 SQ. FT.
BEDROOMS: 5
BATHROOMS: 4 ½ + ½
WIDTH: 106' - 5"
DEPTH: 104' - 2"

SEARCH ONLINE @ EPLANS.COM

Looking a bit like a mountain resort, this fine rustic-style home is sure to be the envy of your neighborhood. Entering through the elegant front door, one finds an open staircase to the right and a spacious great room directly ahead. Here, a fireplace and a wall of windows give a cozy welcome. A lavish master suite begins with a sitting room complete with a fireplace and continues to a private porch, large walk-in closet, and sumptuous bedroom area. The gourmet kitchen adjoins a sunny dining room that offers access to a screened porch.

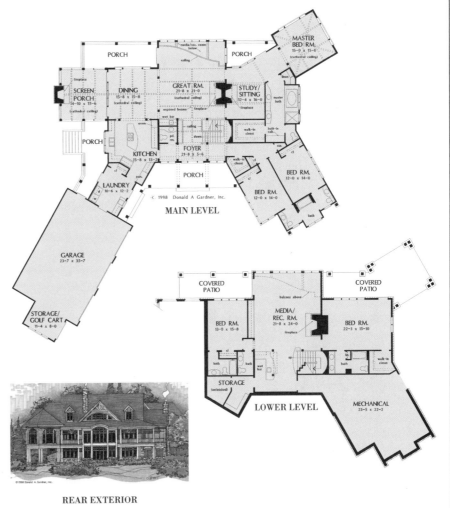

MAIN LEVEL

LOWER LEVEL

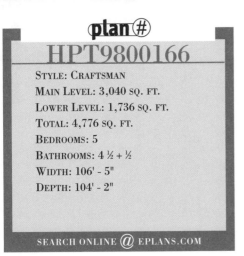

REAR EXTERIOR

The interior of this home boasts high ceilings, a wealth of windows, and interestingly shaped rooms. A covered portico leads into a roomy foyer, which is flanked by an office/study, accessible through French doors. Just beyond the foyer, a huge, vaulted family room highlights columns decorating the entrance and positioned throughout the room. The island kitchen nestles close to the beautiful dining room, which features rear property views through the bay window and a nearby door to the terrace. The main level master suite enjoys two walk-in closets and a lavish bath, as well as access to a covered terrace. The lower level is home to the remaining bedrooms, including Suites 2 and 3, an abundance of storage, a recreation room, and a large mechanical/storage room.

plan #

HPT9800167

STYLE: CRAFTSMAN
MAIN LEVEL: 2,932 SQ. FT.
LOWER LEVEL: 1,556 SQ. FT.
TOTAL: 4,488 SQ. FT.
BEDROOMS: 3
BATHROOMS: 3½ + ½
WIDTH: 114' - 0"
DEPTH: 82' - 11"
FOUNDATION: BASEMENT

SEARCH ONLINE @ EPLANS.COM

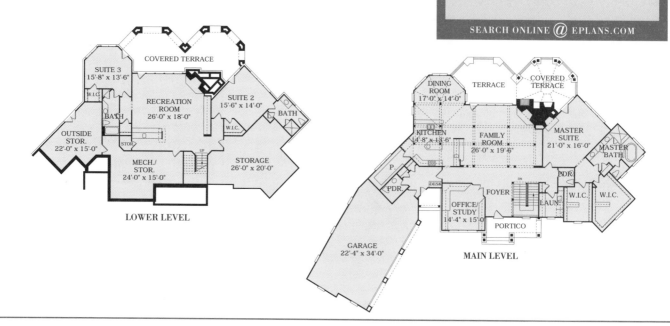

ptan#

HPT9800168

STYLE: COUNTRY COTTAGE
FIRST FLOOR: 1,773 SQ. FT.
SECOND FLOOR: 2,293 SQ. FT.
TOTAL: 4,066 SQ. FT.
BEDROOMS: 5
BATHROOMS: 4½
WIDTH: 69' - 0"
DEPTH: 54' - 4"
FOUNDATION: BASEMENT,
CRAWLSPACE

SEARCH ONLINE @ EPLANS.COM

This a great home for a large, active family that is continually inviting friends over. Five bedrooms, four of them upstairs, offer lots of sleeping space. A large entertainment room is designed for games, music, and movies. On the main floor, a spacious family room with a fireplace and coffered ceiling, and a formal dining room will provide many memorable get-togethers. The study offers a quiet retreat, and the nearby bedroom, which adjoins a full bath, works well as a guest room. The casual eating area flows into the kitchen, which is well-designed for effortless food preparation.

SECOND FLOOR

FIRST FLOOR

This charming home combines hipped rooflines, shingles, and brickwork to create a design with European elements. Enter through the foyer, and to the left is a vaulted dining room with front property views. The gathering room—complete with a fireplace—and living room flank the kitchen. A bayed breakfast nook looks out to the lower rear terrace, and also enjoys close proximity to the kitchen. The first-floor master suite on the right side of the plan includes such amenities as a tray ceiling, His and Hers walk-in closets, a full bath, garden tub, and separate shower. The second floor houses the remaining sleeping quarters. Suites 2 and 4 share a full bath, and each boast a balcony. Suite 3 enjoys a private bath and a walk-in closet. A partially vaulted playroom completes the second floor.

plan #
HPT9800030

STYLE: COUNTRY COTTAGE
FIRST FLOOR: 2,430 SQ. FT.
SECOND FLOOR: 1,624 SQ. FT.
TOTAL: 4,054 SQ. FT.
BEDROOMS: 4
BATHROOMS: 3½ + ½
WIDTH: 70' - 4"
DEPTH: 95' - 9"
FOUNDATION: CRAWLSPACE

SEARCH ONLINE @ EPLANS.COM

FIRST FLOOR

SECOND FLOOR

REAR EXTERIOR

plan #

HPT9800033

STYLE: NORMAN
FIRST FLOOR: 2,267 SQ. FT.
SECOND FLOOR: 2,209 SQ. FT.
TOTAL: 4,476 SQ. FT.
BEDROOMS: 4
BATHROOMS: 3½
WIDTH: 67' - 2"
DEPTH: 64' - 10"
FOUNDATION: CRAWLSPACE

SEARCH ONLINE @ EPLANS.COM

Keystone arches, a wonderful turret, vertical shutters, and decorative stickwork over the entry add to the charm of this fine home. A formal dining room at the front of the plan is complemented by the breakfast bay at the rear. An angled snack bar/counter separates the island kitchen from the gathering room. An adjoining recreation room offers a wet bar and a second flight of stairs to the sleeping quarters. Bay windows brighten the master suite and Suite 2, both with private baths. Two more bedrooms share a full bath that includes a dressing area and twin vanities. The laundry room is on this level for convenience.

SECOND FLOOR

FIRST FLOOR

© 1999 Donald A. Gardner, Inc.

This custom-designed estate home elegantly combines stone and stucco, arched windows, and stunning exterior details under its formidable hipped roof. The two-story foyer is impressive with its grand staircase, tray ceiling, and overlooking balcony. Equally remarkable is the generous living room with a fireplace and a coffered two-story ceiling. The kitchen, breakfast bay, and family room with a fireplace are all open to one another for a comfortable, casual atmosphere. The first-floor master suite indulges with numerous closets, a dressing room, and a fabulous bath. Upstairs, four more bedrooms are topped by tray ceilings—three have walk-in closets and two have private baths. The three-car garage boasts additional storage and a bonus room above.

plan #

HPT9800169

STYLE: FARMHOUSE
FIRST FLOOR: 3,520 SQ. FT.
SECOND FLOOR: 1,638 SQ. FT.
TOTAL: 5,158 SQ. FT.
BONUS SPACE: 411 SQ. FT.
BEDROOMS: 5
BATHROOMS: 4½
WIDTH: 96' - 6"
DEPTH: 58' - 8"

SEARCH ONLINE @ EPLANS.COM

FIRST FLOOR

SECOND FLOOR

plan

HPT9800014

STYLE: NORMAN
FIRST FLOOR: 2,639 SQ. FT.
SECOND FLOOR: 1,625 SQ. FT.
TOTAL: 4,264 SQ. FT.
BEDROOMS: 4
BATHROOMS: 3½
WIDTH: 73' - 8"
DEPTH: 58' - 6"
FOUNDATION: BASEMENT,
CRAWLSPACE, SLAB

SEARCH ONLINE @ EPLANS.COM

This home offers both luxury and practicality. A study and dining room flank the foyer, and the great room offers a warming fireplace and double French-door access to the rear yard. A butler's pantry acts as a helpful buffer between the kitchen and the columned dining room. Double bays at the rear of the home form the keeping room and the breakfast room on one side and the master bedroom on the other. Three family bedrooms and two baths grace the second floor. A game room is perfect for casual family time.

SECOND FLOOR

FIRST FLOOR

REAR EXTERIOR

COPYRIGHT LARRY E. BELK

This majestic storybook cottage, from the magical setting of rural Europe, provides the perfect home for any large family with a wealth of modern comforts within. A graceful staircase cascades from the two-story foyer. To the left, a sophisticated study offers a wall of built-ins. To the right, a formal dining room is easily served from the island kitchen. The breakfast room accesses the rear screened porch. Fireplaces warm the great room and keeping room. Two sets of double doors open from the great room to the rear covered porch. The master bedroom features private porch access, a sitting area, lavish bath, and two walk-in closets. Upstairs, three additional family bedrooms offer walk-in closet space galore! The game room is great entertainment for both family and friends. A three-car garage with golf-cart storage completes the plan.

plan#

HPT9800170

STYLE: EUROPEAN COTTAGE
FIRST FLOOR: 3,033 SQ. FT.
SECOND FLOOR: 1,545 SQ. FT.
TOTAL: 4,578 SQ. FT.
BEDROOMS: 4
BATHROOMS: 3½ + ½
WIDTH: 91' - 6"
DEPTH: 63' - 8"
FOUNDATION: BASEMENT, CRAWLSPACE, SLAB

SEARCH ONLINE @ EPLANS.COM

FIRST FLOOR

SECOND FLOOR

plan #

HPT9800171

STYLE: MEDITERRANEAN

FIRST FLOOR: 5,120 SQ. FT.

SECOND FLOOR: 880 SQ. FT.

TOTAL: 6,000 SQ. FT.

BEDROOMS: 5

BATHROOMS: 6½

WIDTH: 91' - 0"

DEPTH: 132' - 0"

FOUNDATION: CRAWLSPACE

SEARCH ONLINE @ EPLANS.COM

This sprawling Mediterranean estate is rich with the amenities and extra touches that make a luxurious house a home. Three entrances allow guests to come through the formal entry and family members to use the courtyard or rear porch. Ceilings throughout are 10 feet or higher, for grandeur at every turn. The dining room leads to the gourmet kitchen, complete with an island cooktop and plenty of workspace. An adjacent two-story eating area is perfect for casual meals. The sewing room and gym announce three vaulted bedroom suites in an intriguing layout. The master suite is secluded for privacy in the opposite wing. Here, His and Hers closets and a sumptuous bath with an angled tub and a bidet are sure to please. Upstairs, the piano gallery and guest room open to the two-story rear porch.

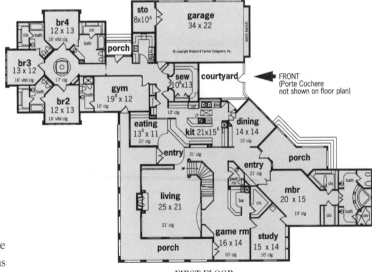

FIRST FLOOR

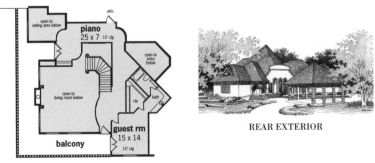

SECOND FLOOR

REAR EXTERIOR

VERANDA

SCREENED PORCH 13'-0" x 17'-0"

BREAKFAST 14'-0" x 8'-0"

KITCHEN 17'-6" x 19'-6"

GATHERING ROOM 24'-0" x 18'-0"

SITTING 13'-6" x 8'-0"

MASTER SUITE 19'-6" x 13'-0"

LAUN.

GALLERY

MED. RM.

PDR.

DINING ROOM 12'-0" x 13'-6"

FOYER

HIS

HERS

OFFICE

STOR.

MASTER BATH

GARAGE 23'-0" x 22'-4"

PORCH

FIRST FLOOR

SUITE 3 17'-2" x 17'-0"

BATH

W.I.C.

OPEN TO BELOW

BALCONY

STUDY LOFT 8'-10" x 11'-0"

W.I.C.

DRESS.

SUITE 2 12'-6" x 14'-2"

OPEN BELOW

BATH

SUITE 4 / BONUS RM 16'-2" x 23'-0"

SECOND FLOOR

COVERED VERANDA

OFFICE 12'-0" x 11'-6"

COVERED VERANDA

EXERCISE ROOM 13'-0" x 13'-2"

BATH

RECREATION ROOM 32'-0" x 23'-0"

GARAGE 20'-0" x 23'-6"

STOR. 10'-10" x 13'-0"

BAR 10'-4" x 10'-6"

WINE

MECH./ STOR.

BASEMENT

plan
HPT9800172

STYLE: FRENCH COUNTRY
FIRST FLOOR: 2,734 SQ. FT.
SECOND FLOOR: 1,605 SQ. FT.
TOTAL: 4,339 SQ. FT.
BONUS SPACE: 391 SQ. FT.
BASEMENT: 1,701 SQ. FT.
BEDROOMS: 4
BATHROOMS: 4½
WIDTH: 88' - 0"
DEPTH: 92' - 8"
FOUNDATION: BASEMENT

SEARCH ONLINE @ EPLANS.COM

Attractive stone, curved dormers, and varied rooflines give this fine European manor a graceful dose of class. Inside, the foyer introduces a formal dining room defined by columns and a spacious gathering room with a fireplace. The nearby kitchen features a walk-in pantry, beamed ceiling, adjacent breakfast nook, and a screened porch. The first-floor master suite features two walk-in closets, a lavish bath, a corner fireplace, and a sitting room with access to the rear veranda. Upstairs, three suites offer walk-in closets and surround a study loft. On the lower level, a huge recreation room awaits to entertain with a bar, a fireplace and outdoor access. A secluded office provides a private entrance—perfect for a home business.

REAR EXTERIOR

plan #

HPT9800173

STYLE: COUNTRY COTTAGE

FIRST FLOOR: 3,248 SQ. FT.

SECOND FLOOR: 1,426 SQ. FT.

TOTAL: 4,674 SQ. FT.

BEDROOMS: 5

BATHROOMS: 5½ + ½

WIDTH: 99' - 10"

DEPTH: 74' - 10"

FOUNDATION: BASEMENT

SEARCH ONLINE @ EPLANS.COM

Multiple rooflines; a stone, brick, and siding facade; and an absolutely grand entrance combine to give this home the look of luxury. A striking family room showcases a beautiful fireplace framed with built-ins. The nearby breakfast room streams with light and accesses the rear patio. The kitchen features an island workstation, walk-in pantry, and plenty of counter space. A guest suite is available on the first floor, perfect for when family members visit. The first-floor master suite enjoys easy access to a large study, bayed sitting room, and luxurious bath. Private baths are also included for each of the upstairs bedrooms.

SECOND FLOOR

FIRST FLOOR

plan
HPT9800022

STYLE: MEDITERRANEAN
SQUARE FOOTAGE: 4,222
BONUS SPACE: 590 SQ. FT.
BEDROOMS: 4
BATHROOMS: 5
WIDTH: 83' - 10"
DEPTH: 112' - 0"
FOUNDATION: SLAB

SEARCH ONLINE @ EPLANS.COM

The striking facade of this magnificent estate is just the beginning of the excitement you will encounter inside. The foyer passes the formal dining room on the way to the columned gallery. The formal living room opens to the rear patio and has easy access to a wet bar. The contemporary kitchen has a work island and all the amenities for gourmet preparation. The family room will be a favorite for casual entertainment. The family sleeping wing begins with an octagonal vestibule and has three bedrooms with private baths. The master wing features a private garden and an opulent bath.

plan #

HPT9800174

STYLE: CONTEMPORARY
FIRST FLOOR: 4,066 SQ. FT.
SECOND FLOOR: 591 SQ. FT.
TOTAL: 4,657 SQ. FT.
BEDROOMS: 3
BATHROOMS: 3
WIDTH: 109' - 0"
DEPTH: 73' - 4"
FOUNDATION: CRAWLSPACE

SEARCH ONLINE @ EPLANS.COM

Warm brick makes an intriguing statement on this refreshing Greco-Roman-inspired home. In the foyer, a barrel vault makes a grand entrance. The formal dining room is accented with columns and arches. A central planter brings in natural beauty year-round. Step down to a sunken living room with a fireplace and balcony overlook from above. Surrounding windows let the sunshine flow in. A media room and wet bar are great for entertaining. The master suite enjoys a private covered patio, decadent bath and His and Hers walk-in closets.

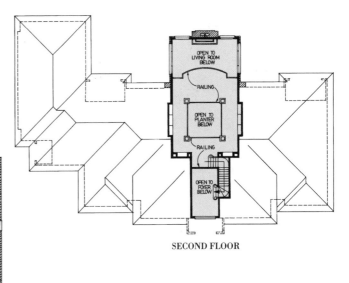

SECOND FLOOR

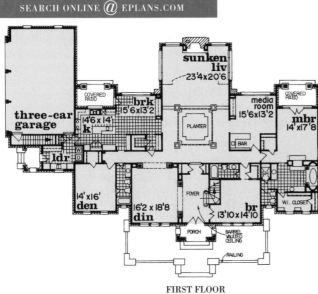

FIRST FLOOR

This captivating luxury home puts a contemporary spin on Old World style. Stucco provides a wonderful complement to multiple arched windows on the exterior; inside, natural light streams into the two-story entry. Just ahead, the living room is graced with a rear window bay and a warming fireplace. The professional-grade kitchen is ready to serve the elegant dining room and bright breakfast nook, both set in bays. A built-in entertainment center in the family room gives the space a definite focus. The right wing is devoted to the master suite: a bayed window lets in the light, as the dazzling bath soothes with a whirlpool tub and room-size walk-in closet. Follow the U-shaped staircase to a mid-level study; three grand bedrooms, a lofty game room and a sundeck complete the plan.

plan #
HPT9800175

STYLE: CONTEMPORARY
FIRST FLOOR: 2,489 SQ. FT.
SECOND FLOOR: 1,650 SQ. FT.
TOTAL: 4,139 SQ. FT.
BONUS SPACE: 366 SQ. FT.
BEDROOMS: 4
BATHROOMS: 3½
WIDTH: 72' - 8"
DEPTH: 77' - 0"

SEARCH ONLINE @ EPLANS.COM

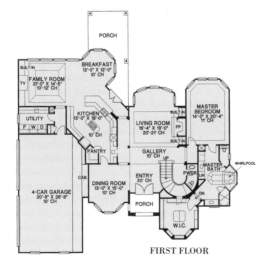

FIRST FLOOR

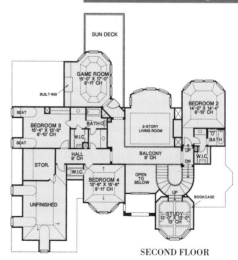

SECOND FLOOR

Ideal Golf Course Home

QUOTE ONE®
Cost to build? See page 187
to order complete cost estimate
to build this house in your area!

plan #
HPT9800176

STYLE: MEDITERRANEAN
FIRST FLOOR: 3,350 SQ. FT.
SECOND FLOOR: 1,298 SQ. FT.
TOTAL: 4,648 SQ. FT.
BEDROOMS: 5
BATHROOMS: 3½ + ½
WIDTH: 97' - 0"
DEPTH: 74' - 4"
FOUNDATION: BASEMENT

SEARCH ONLINE @ EPLANS.COM

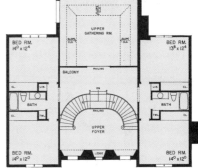
SECOND FLOOR

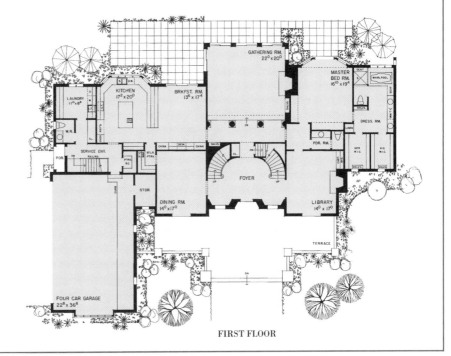
FIRST FLOOR

Reminiscent of a Mediterranean villa, this grand manor is a showstopper on the outside and a comfortable residence on the inside. An elegant receiving hall boasts a double staircase and is flanked by the formal dining room and the library. A huge gathering room at the back is graced by a fireplace and a wall of sliding glass doors to the rear terrace. The master bedroom resides on the first floor for privacy. With a lavish bath to pamper you and His and Hers walk-in closets, this suite will be a delight to retire to each evening. Upstairs are four additional bedrooms with ample storage space, a large balcony overlooking the gathering room, and two full baths.

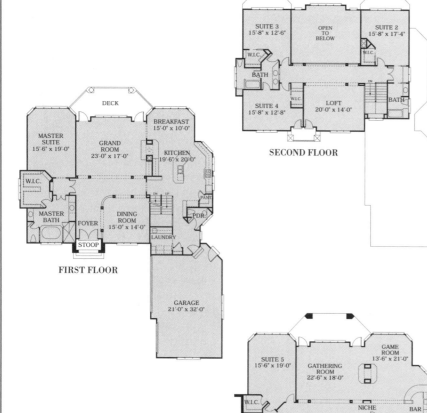

DECK

MASTER SUITE 15'-6" x 19'-0"

GRAND ROOM 23'-0" x 17'-0"

BREAKFAST 15'-0" x 10'-0"

KITCHEN 19'-6" x 20'-0"

W.I.C.

MASTER BATH

FOYER

DINING ROOM 15'-0" x 14'-0"

PANT.

PDR.

LAUNDRY

STOOP

FIRST FLOOR

GARAGE 21'-0" x 32'-0"

SUITE 3 15'-8" x 12'-6"

OPEN TO BELOW

SUITE 2 15'-8" x 17'-4"

W.I.C.

BATH

W.I.C.

SUITE 4 15'-8" x 12'-8"

W.I.C.

LOFT 20'-0" x 14'-0"

DN

BATH

SECOND FLOOR

SUITE 5 15'-6" x 19'-0"

GATHERING ROOM 22'-6" x 18'-0"

GAME ROOM 13'-6" x 21'-0"

W.I.C.

BATH

NICHE

BAR

UP

UNFIN.

BASEMENT

plan #

HPT9800011

STYLE: PRAIRIE
FIRST FLOOR: 2,450 SQ. FT.
SECOND FLOOR: 1,674 SQ. FT.
TOTAL: 4,124 SQ. FT.
BASEMENT: 1,568 SQ. FT.
BEDROOMS: 4
BATHROOMS: 3½
WIDTH: 65' - 10"
DEPTH: 85' - 2"
FOUNDATION: BASEMENT

SEARCH ONLINE @ EPLANS.COM

This sensational bungalow borrows exquisite details from the Craftsman style. The rustic texture of the building materials, broad overhangs, and second-floor shingles call up a brilliant architectural era. Inside, an open arrangement of dining and living space allows shared views, impeded only by lovely decorative columns. The gourmet kitchen shares a through-fireplace with the grand room and serves a breakfast area. The master suite occupies the entire left wing; three family bedroom suites reside upstairs.

ptan

HPT9800177

STYLE: MEDITERRANEAN
MAIN LEVEL: 2,391 SQ. FT.
UPPER LEVEL: 922 SQ. FT.
LOWER LEVEL: 1,964 SQ. FT.
TOTAL: 5,277 SQ. FT.
BONUS SPACE: 400 SQ. FT.
BEDROOMS: 4
BATHROOMS: 4½
WIDTH: 63' - 10"
DEPTH: 85' - 6"
FOUNDATION: BASEMENT

SEARCH ONLINE @ EPLANS.COM

Here's an upscale multilevel plan with expansive rear views. The first floor provides an open living and dining area, defined by decorative columns and enhanced by natural light from tall windows. A breakfast area with a lovely triple window opens to a sunroom, which allows light to pour into the gourmet kitchen. The master wing features a tray ceiling in the bedroom, two walk-in closets, and an elegant private vestibule leading to a lavish bath. Upstairs, a reading loft overlooks the great room and leads to a sleeping area with two suites. A recreation room, exercise room, office, guest suite, and additional storage are available in the finished basement.

UPPER LEVEL

MAIN LEVEL

LOWER LEVEL

REAR EXTERIOR

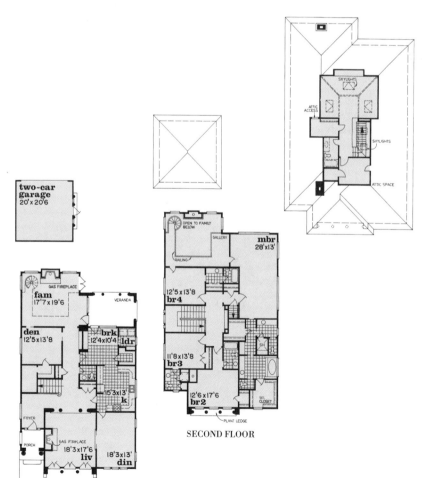

FIRST FLOOR

two-car garage 20'x20'6

fam 17'7 x 19'6

VERANDA

GAS FIREPLACE

den 12'5 x 13'8

brk 12'4 x 10'4

ldr

k

15'3 x 13'

FOYER

PORCH

GAS FIREPLACE

liv 18'3 x 17'6

din 18'3 x 13'

TERRACE

SECOND FLOOR

OPEN TO FAMILY BELOW

GALLERY

RAILING

mbr 28'x13'

br4 12'5 x 13'8

br3 11'8 x 13'8

br2 12'6 x 17'6

W.I. CLOSET

SH

PLANT LEDGE

SKYLIGHTS

ATTIC ACCESS

SKYLIGHTS

ATTIC SPACE

plan #

HPT9800178

STYLE: CONTEMPORARY
FIRST FLOOR: 2,196 SQ. FT.
SECOND FLOOR: 2,246 SQ. FT.
TOTAL: 4,442 SQ. FT.
BONUS SPACE: 673 SQ. FT.
BEDROOMS: 4
BATHROOMS: 4½
WIDTH: 40' - 0"
DEPTH: 74' - 6"
FOUNDATION: BASEMENT

SEARCH ONLINE @ EPLANS.COM

A contemporary classic with Mediterranean flair, this beautiful home will be the envy of any community. Follow the formal foyer to the right, where an elegant living room is graced with columns, a gas fireplace, and triplet French doors topped by sunbursts, leading out to the terrace. A private den includes storage space, making it a great home office. In the casual family room, a gas fireplace warms and saves energy. A spiral staircase leads to the balcony overlook above and the family quarters. Three bedroom suites enjoy private baths; the master suite is full of natural light and relishes an indulgent bath. A second staircase leads back down to the foyer.

plan
HPT9800036

STYLE: CHATEAU STYLE
FIRST FLOOR: 3,517 SQ. FT.
SECOND FLOOR: 1,254 SQ. FT.
TOTAL: 4,771 SQ. FT.
BEDROOMS: 5
BATHROOMS: 4½ + ½
WIDTH: 95' - 8"
DEPTH: 107' - 0"
FOUNDATION: SLAB

SEARCH ONLINE @ EPLANS.COM

The design of this French Country estate captures its ambiance with its verandas, grand entry, and unique balconies. A spectacular panorama of the formal living areas and the elegant curved stairway awaits just off the foyer. A large island kitchen, breakfast nook, and family room will impress, as will the wine cellar. Plenty of kitchen pantry space leads to the laundry and motor court featuring a two-car garage attached to the main house and a three-car garage attached by a breezeway. The master suite boasts a sunken sitting area with a see-through fireplace, His and Hers walk-in closets, island tub, and large separate shower. A study area, three additional bedrooms, a full bath, and a bonus area reside on the second floor.

FIRST FLOOR

SECOND FLOOR

Finished with French Country adornments, this estate home is comfortable in just about any setting. Main living areas are sunk down just a bit from the entry foyer, providing them with soaring ceilings and sweeping views. The family room features a focal fireplace. A columned entry gains access to the master suite where separate sitting and sleeping areas are defined by a three-sided fireplace. There are three bedrooms upstairs; one has a private bath. The sunken media room on this level includes storage space. Look for the decks on the second level.

plan #

HPT9800004

STYLE: FRENCH
FIRST FLOOR: 2,899 SQ. FT.
SECOND FLOOR: 1,472 SQ. FT.
TOTAL: 4,371 SQ. FT.
BEDROOMS: 4
BATHROOMS: 3½
WIDTH: 69' - 4"
DEPTH: 76' - 8"
FOUNDATION: SLAB

SEARCH ONLINE @ EPLANS.COM

FIRST FLOOR

SECOND FLOOR

OPTIONAL LAYOUT

eplans.com

THE GATEWAY TO YOUR NEW HOME

Looking for more plans? Got questions?
Try our one-stop home plans resource—eplans.com.

We'll help you streamline the plan selection process, so your dreams can become reality faster than you ever imagined. From choosing your home plan and ideal location to finding an experienced contractor, eplans.com will guide you every step of the way.

Mix and match! Explore! At eplans.com you can combine all your top criteria to find your perfect match. Search for your ideal home plan by any or all of the following:
> Number of bedrooms or baths,
> Total square feet,
> House style,
> Designer, and
> Cost.

With over 10,000 plans, the options are endless. Colonial, ranch, country, and Victorian are just a few of the house styles offered. Keep in mind your essential lifestyle features—whether to include a porch, fireplace, bonus room, or main-floor laundry room. And the garage—how many cars must it accommodate, if any? By filling out the preference page on eplans.com, we'll help you narrow your search.

At eplans.com we'll make the building process a snap to understand. At the click of a button you'll find a complete building guide. And our eplans task planner will create a construction calendar just for you. Here you'll find links to tips and other valuable information to help you every step of the way—from choosing a site to moving day.

For your added convenience, our home plans experts are available for live, one-on-one chats at eplans.com. Building a home may seem like a complicated project, but it doesn't have to be—particularly if you'll let us help you from start to finish.

COPYRIGHT DOS & DON'TS

Blueprints for residential construction (or working drawings, as they are often called in the industry) are copyrighted intellectual property, protected under the terms of United States Copyright Law and, therefore, cannot be copied legally for use in building. However, we've made it easy for you to get what you need to build your home, without violating copyright law. Following are some guidelines to help you obtain the right number of copies for your chosen blueprint design.

COPYRIGHT DO

■ Do purchase enough copies of the blueprints to satisfy building requirements. As a rule for a home or project plan, you will need a set for yourself, two or three for your builder and subcontractors, two for the local building department, and one to three for your mortgage lender. You may want to check with your local building department or your builder to see how many they need before you purchase. You may need to buy eight to 10 sets; note that some areas of the country require purchase of vellums (also called reproducibles) instead of blueprints. Vellums can be written on and changed more easily than blueprints. Also, remember, plans are only good for one-time construction.

■ Do consider reverse blueprints if you want to flop the plan. Lettering and numbering will appear backward, but the reversed sets will help you and your builder better visualize the design.

■ Do take advantage of multiple-set discounts at the time you place your order. Usually, purchasing additional sets after you receive your initial order is not as cost-effective.

■ Do take advantage of vellums. Though they are a little more expensive, they can be changed, copied, and used for one-time construction of a home. You will receive a copyright release letter with your vellums that will allow you to have them copied.

■ Do talk with one of our professional service representatives before placing your order. They can give you great advice about what packages are available for your chosen design and what will work best for your particular situation.

COPYRIGHT DON'T

■ Don't think you should purchase only one set of blueprints for a building project. One is fine if you want to study the plan closely, but will not be enough for actual building.

■ Don't expect your builder or a copy center to make copies of standard blueprints. They cannot legally—most copy centers are aware of this.

■ Don't purchase standard blueprints if you know you'll want to make changes to the plans; vellums are a better value.

■ Don't use blueprints or vellums more than one time. Additional fees apply if you want to build more than one time from a set of drawings. ■

hanley▲wood
HomePlanners

ORDERING IS EASY

HANLEY WOOD HOMEPLANNERS HAS EVERYTHING YOU NEED TO BUILD THE home of your dreams, and with more than 50 years of experience in the industry, we make it as easy as possible for you to reach those goals. Just follow the steps on these pages and you'll receive a high-quality, ready-to-build set of home blueprints, plus everything else you need to make your home-building effort a success.

WHERE TO BEGIN?
1. CHOOSE YOUR PLAN

■ Browsing magazines, books, and eplans.com can be an exciting and rewarding part of the home-building process. As you search, make a list of the things you want in your dream home—everything from number of bedrooms and baths to details like fireplaces or a home office.

■ Take the time to consider your lot and your neighborhood, and how the home you choose will fit with both. And think about the future—how might your needs change if you plan to live in this house for five, 10, or 20 years?

■ With thousands of plans available, chances are that you'll have no trouble discovering your dream home. If you find something that's almost perfect, our Customization Program can help make it exactly what you want.

■ Most important, be sure to enjoy the process of picking out your new home!

WHAT YOU'LL GET WITH YOUR ORDER

Each designer's blueprint set is unique, but they all provide everything you'll need to build your home. Here are some standard elements you can expect to find in your plans:

1. FRONT PERSPECTIVE
This artist's sketch of the exterior of the house gives you an idea of how the house will look when built and landscaped.

2. FOUNDATION PLANS
This sheet shows the foundation layout including support walls, excavated and unexcavated areas, if any, and foundation notes. If your plan features slab construction rather than a basement, the plan shows footings and details for a monolithic slab. This page, or another in the set, may include a sample plot plan for locating your house on a building site.

3. DETAILED FLOOR PLANS
These plans show the layout of each floor of the house. Rooms and interior spaces are carefully dimensioned and keys are given for cross-section details provided later in the plans. The positions of electrical outlets and switches are shown.

4. HOUSE CROSS-SECTIONS
Large-scale views show sections or cutaways of the foundation, interior walls, exterior walls, floors, stairways, and roof details. Additional cross-sections may show important changes in floor, ceiling, or roof heights, or the relationship of one level to another. Extremely valuable during construction, these sections show exactly how the various parts of the house fit together.

5. INTERIOR ELEVATIONS
These elevations, or drawings, show the design and placement of kitchen and bathroom cabinets, laundry areas, fireplaces, bookcases, and other built-ins. Little extras, such as mantelpiece and wainscoting drawings, plus molding sections, provide details that give your home that custom touch.

6. EXTERIOR ELEVATIONS
Every blueprint set comes with drawings of the front exterior, and may include the rear and sides of your house as well. These drawings give necessary notes on exterior materials and finishes. Particular attention is given to cornice detail, brick, and stone accents or other finish items that make your home unique.

GETTING DOWN TO BUSINESS
2. PRICE YOUR PLAN

HANLEY WOOD
HOMEPLANNERS
ADVANTAGE
ORDER 24 HOURS!
1-800-521-6797

BLUEPRINT PRICE SCHEDULE

PRICE TIERS	1-SET STUDY PACKAGE	4-SET BUILDING PACKAGE	8-SET BUILDING PACKAGE	1-SET REPRODUCIBLE*
P1	$20	$50	$90	$140
P2	$40	$70	$110	$160
P3	$70	$100	$140	$190
P4	$100	$130	$170	$220
P5	$140	$170	$210	$270
P6	$180	$210	$250	$310
A1	$440	$490	$540	$660
A2	$480	$530	$580	$720
A3	$530	$590	$650	$800
A4	$575	$645	$705	$870
C1	$625	$695	$755	$935
C2	$670	$740	$800	$1000
C3	$715	$790	$855	$1075
C4	$765	$840	$905	$1150
L1	$870	$965	$1050	$1300
L2	$945	$1040	$1125	$1420
L3	$1050	$1150	$1240	$1575
L4	$1155	$1260	$1355	$1735
SQ1				.35/SQ. FT.

PRICES SUBJECT TO CHANGE

* REQUIRES A FAX NUMBER

plan ⊕
READY TO ORDER

Once you've found your plan, get your plan number and turn to the following pages to find its price tier. Use the corresponding code and the Blueprint Price Schedule above to determine your price for a variety of blueprint packages.

Keep in mind that you'll need multiple sets to fulfill building requirements, and only reproducible sets may be altered or duplicated.

To the right you'll find prices for additional and reverse blueprint sets. Also note in the following pages whether your home has a corresponding Deck or Landscape Plan, and whether you can order our Quote One® cost-to-build information or a Materials List for your plan.

IT'S EASY TO ORDER
JUST VISIT
EPLANS.COM OR CALL
TOLL-FREE
1-800-521-6797

PRICE SCHEDULE FOR ADDITIONAL OPTIONS

OPTIONS FOR PLANS IN TIERS P1-P6	COSTS
ADDITIONAL IDENTICAL BLUEPRINTS FOR "P1-P6" PLANS	$10 PER SET
REVERSE BLUEPRINTS (MIRROR IMAGE) FOR "P1-P6" PLANS	$10 FEE PER ORDER
1 SET OF DECK CONSTRUCTION DETAILS	$14.95 EACH
DECK CONSTRUCTION PACKAGE (INCLUDES 1 SET OF "P1-P6" PLANS, PLUS 1 SET STANDARD DECK CONSTRUCTION DETAILS)	ADD $10 TO BUILDING PACKAGE PRICE

OPTIONS FOR PLANS IN TIERS A1-SQ1	COSTS
ADDITIONAL IDENTICAL BLUEPRINTS IN SAME ORDER FOR "A1-L4" PLANS	$50 PER SET
REVERSE BLUEPRINTS (MIRROR IMAGE) WITH 4- OR 8-SET ORDER FOR "A1-L4" PLANS	$50 FEE PER ORDER
SPECIFICATION OUTLINES	$10 EACH
MATERIALS LISTS FOR "A1-C3" PLANS	$70 EACH
MATERIALS LISTS FOR "C4-SQ1" PLANS	$70 EACH

IMPORTANT EXTRAS	COSTS
ELECTRICAL, PLUMBING, CONSTRUCTION, AND MECHANICAL DETAIL SETS	$14.95 EACH; ANY TWO $22.95; ANY THREE $29.95; ALL FOUR $39.95
HOME FURNITURE PLANNER	$15.95 EACH
REAR ELEVATION	$10 EACH
QUOTE ONE® SUMMARY COST REPORT	$29.95
QUOTE ONE® DETAILED COST ESTIMATE (FOR MORE DETAILS ABOUT QUOTE ONE®, SEE STEP 3.)	$60

IMPORTANT NOTE
Source Key

■ THE 1-SET STUDY PACKAGE IS MARKED "NOT FOR CONSTRUCTION."

HPT98

PLAN #	PRICE TIER	PAGE	MATERIALS LIST	QUOTE ONE®	DECK	DECK PRICE	LANDSCAPE	LANDSCAPE PRICE	REGIONS
HPT9800001	C4	83							
HPT9800002	C4	122							
HPT9800003	C1	37	Y						
HPT9800004	SQ1	180							
HPT9800005	L1	144							
HPT9800007	SQ1	18							
HPT9800008	SQ1	135	Y						
HPT9800009	C3	93							
HPT9800010	A4	57							
HPT9800011	C4	176							
HPT9800012	C3	155							
HPT9800013	L1	145							
HPT9800014	L1	167					OLA008	P4	1234568
HPT9800015	C2	53	Y	Y					
HPT9800016	C3	90							
HPT9800017	SQ1	17							
HPT9800018	C3	123	Y						
HPT9800019	C4	124							
HPT9800020	SQ1	27							
HPT9800021	C3	79							
HPT9800022	SQ1	172	Y						
HPT9800023	C2	49							
HPT9800024	C2	44	Y						
HPT9800025	SQ1	157	Y						
HPT9800026	C2	114	Y				OLA015	P4	123568
HPT9800027	C2	126	Y						
HPT9800028	C1	35	Y	Y					
HPT9800029	C2	125	Y						
HPT9800030	L2	164							
HPT9800031	SQ1	75	Y						
HPT9800032	SQ1	116	Y						
HPT9800033	L2	165							
HPT9800035	C2	85	Y	Y	ODA012	P3	OLA024	P4	123568
HPT9800036	SQ1	179							
HPT9800037	C4	130	Y						
HPT9800038	C3	115	Y						
HPT9800039	C3	88							
HPT9800040	C3	105	Y	Y					
HPT9800041	C3	5							
HPT9800042	SQ1	6							
HPT9800043	C2	7							
HPT9800044	C4	8	Y						
HPT9800045	SQ1	9							
HPT9800046	A4	10							
HPT9800047	C1	11	Y						
HPT9800048	C2	12	Y						
HPT9800049	L1	13							
HPT9800050	C4	14							
HPT9800051	L1	15	Y	Y	ODA008	P3	OLA016	P4	1234568
HPT9800052	C2	16	Y	Y			OLA001	P3	123568
HPT9800053	C2	19							
HPT9800054	C3	20							
HPT9800055	SQ1	21	Y						
HPT9800056	C1	22	Y						
HPT9800057	C2	23							
HPT9800058	SQ1	24							
HPT9800059	L1	25	Y	Y					
HPT9800060	SQ1	26	Y						
HPT9800061	C2	28							
HPT9800062	SQ1	29	Y						
HPT9800063	L2	30							
HPT9800064	C2	31	Y	Y					
HPT9800065	C2	32	Y	Y					
HPT9800066	C2	33							
HPT9800067	C2	34							
HPT9800068	C1	36	Y		ODA012	P3	OLA010	P3	1234568
HPT9800069	A4	38	Y						
HPT9800070	C1	39	Y						
HPT9800071	C1	40	Y						
HPT9800072	C2	41	Y						
HPT9800073	A4	42	Y	Y			OLA001	P3	123568
HPT9800074	A4	43	Y						
HPT9800075	A4	45	Y						
HPT9800076	A4	46	Y	Y	ODA017	P2	OLA010	P3	1234568
HPT9800077	C2	47	Y	Y	ODA013	P2	OLA018	P3	12345678
HPT9800078	A4	48	Y						
HPT9800079	A4	50							
HPT9800080	A4	51							
HPT9800081	C2	52	Y						
HPT9800082	A4	54							
HPT9800083	A4	55							
HPT9800084	A4	56							
HPT9800085	C1	58							
HPT9800086	C1	59	Y						
HPT9800087	A4	60							
HPT9800088	A4	61	Y	Y			OLA013	P4	12345678
HPT9800089	A4	62	Y						
HPT9800090	C1	63	Y						
HPT9800091	A4	64							
HPT9800092	A4	65	Y						

PLAN #	PRICE TIER	PAGE	MATERIALS LIST	QUOTE ONE®	DECK	DECK PRICE	LANDSCAPE	LANDSCAPE PRICE	REGIONS
HPT9800093	C1	66	Y						
HPT9800094	C1	67	Y						
HPT9800095	A4	68							
HPT9800096	C1	69	Y						
HPT9800097	C1	70	Y						
HPT9800098	C1	71	Y						
HPT9800099	C1	72	Y						
HPT9800100	C1	73	Y						
HPT9800101	C2	74							
HPT9800102	C2	76	Y						
HPT9800103	C2	77	Y						
HPT9800104	C2	78	Y	Y			OLA039	P3	347
HPT9800105	C3	80							
HPT9800106	C2	81	Y						
HPT9800107	C3	82							
HPT9800108	C1	84							
HPT9800109	C1	86							
HPT9800110	C2	87	Y	Y	ODA011	P2	OLA025	P3	123568
HPT9800111	C1	89							
HPT9800112	C3	91							
HPT9800113	C2	92	Y						
HPT9800114	SQ1	94	Y	Y					
HPT9800115	C2	95	Y						
HPT9800116	C3	96							
HPT9800117	SQ1	97							
HPT9800118	C2	98	Y						
HPT9800119	C2	99							
HPT9800120	C1	100							
HPT9800121	C2	101	Y						
HPT9800122	C3	102							
HPT9800123	C1	103	Y						
HPT9800124	C1	104							
HPT9800125	C2	106	Y	Y	ODA012	P3	OLA018	P3	12345678
HPT9800126	C2	107	Y	Y			OLA018	P3	12345678
HPT9800127	C2	108	Y						
HPT9800128	C3	109							
HPT9800129	C1	110					OLA001	P3	123568
HPT9800130	C4	111					OLA004	P3	123568
HPT9800131	SQ1	112	Y						
HPT9800132	C3	113							
HPT9800133	C2	117	Y						
HPT9800134	SQ1	118	Y						
HPT9800135	C4	119							
HPT9800136	C4	120							
HPT9800137	C3	121	Y	Y			OLA024	P4	123568
HPT9800138	C3	127							
HPT9800139	C2	128							
HPT9800140	C2	129	Y						
HPT9800141	C4	131							
HPT9800142	C3	132	Y						
HPT9800143	SQ1	133	Y				OLA008	P4	1234568
HPT9800144	C3	134	Y	Y			OLA038	P3	7
HPT9800145	C2	136	Y	Y			OLA038	P3	7
HPT9800146	SQ1	137	Y						
HPT9800147	L1	138							
HPT9800148	C3	139	Y						
HPT9800149	SQ1	140							
HPT9800150	C3	141							
HPT9800151	C3	142							
HPT9800152	C3	143							
HPT9800153	L1	146							
HPT9800154	L1	147							
HPT9800155	SQ1	148	Y						
HPT9800156	SQ1	149							
HPT9800157	L1	150	Y						
HPT9800158	C3	151	Y						
HPT9800159	SQ1	152							
HPT9800160	SQ1	153							
HPT9800161	L2	154							
HPT9800162	L1	156							
HPT9800163	C4	158	Y						
HPT9800164	L1	159							
HPT9800165	L2	160	Y						
HPT9800166	SQ1	161	Y						
HPT9800167	L2	162							
HPT9800168	L2	163							
HPT9800169	L2	166	Y						
HPT9800170	C4	168							
HPT9800171	L2	169	Y						
HPT9800172	L2	170							
HPT9800173	SQ1	171							
HPT9800174	C4	173							
HPT9800175	L2	174	Y						
HPT9800176	L1	175	Y	Y					
HPT9800177	SQ1	177	Y						
HPT9800178	C4	178							

ORDER ONLINE AT EPLANS.COM

WE OFFER A VARIETY OF USEFUL TOOLS THAT CAN HELP YOU THROUGH EVERY STEP OF THE home-building process. From our Materials List to our Customization Program, these items let you put our experience to work for you to ensure that you get exactly what you want out of your dream house.

MATERIALS LIST

For many of the designs in our portfolio, we offer a customized list of materials that helps you plan and estimate the cost of your new home. The Materials List outlines the quantity, type, and size of materials needed to build your house (with the exception of mechanical system items). Included are framing lumber, windows and doors, kitchen and bath cabinetry, rough and finished hardware, and much more. This handy list helps you or your builder cost out materials and serves as a reference sheet when you're compiling bids.

SPECIFICATION OUTLINE

This valuable 16-page document can play an important role in the construction of your house. Fill it in with your builder, and you'll have a step-by-step chronicle of 166 stages or items crucial to the building process. It provides a comprehensive review of the construction process and helps you choose materials.

QUOTE ONE®

The Quote One® system, which helps estimate the cost of building select designs in your zip code, is available in two parts: the Summary Cost Report and the Material Cost Report.

The Summary Cost Report, the first element in the package, breaks down the cost of your home into various categories based on building materials, labor, and installation, and includes three grades of construction: Budget, Standard, and Custom. Make even more informed decisions about your project with the second element of our package, the Material Cost Report. The material and installation cost is shown for each of more than 1,000 line items provided in the standard-grade Materials List, which is included with this tool. Additional space is included for estimates from contractors and subcontractors, such as for mechanical materials, which are not included in our packages.

If you are interested in a plan that does not indicate the availability of Quote One®, please call and ask our sales representatives, who can verify the status for you.

CUSTOMIZATION PROGRAM

If the plan you love needs something changed to make it perfect, our customization experts will ensure that you get nothing less than your dream home. Purchase a reproducible set of plans for the home you choose, and we'll send you our easy-to-use customization request form via e-mail or fax. For just $50, our customization experts will provide an estimate for your requested revisions, and once it's approved, that charge will be applied to your changes. You'll receive either five sets or a reproducible master of your modified design and any other options you select.

BUILDING BASICS

If you want to know more about building techniques—and deal more confidently with your subcontractors—we offer four useful detail sheets. These sheets provide non-plan-specific general information, but are excellent tools that will add to your understanding of Plumbing Details, Electrical Details, Construction Details, and Mechanical Details. These fact-filled sheets will help answer many of your building questions, and help you learn what questions to ask your builder and subcontractors.

HANDS-ON HOME FURNITURE PLANNER

Effectively plan the space in your home using our Hands-On Home Furniture Planner. It's fun and easy—no more moving heavy pieces of furniture to see how the room will go together. The kit includes reusable peel-and-stick furniture templates that fit on a 12"x18" laminated layout board—enough space to lay out every room in your house.

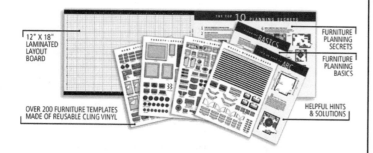

12" X 18" LAMINATED LAYOUT BOARD

FURNITURE PLANNING SECRETS

FURNITURE PLANNING BASICS

HELPFUL HINTS & SOLUTIONS

OVER 200 FURNITURE TEMPLATES MADE OF REUSABLE CLING VINYL

DECK BLUEPRINT PACKAGE

Many of the homes in this book can be enhanced with a professionally designed Home Planners Deck Plan. Those plans marked with a **D** have a corresponding deck plan, sold separately, which includes a Deck Plan Frontal Sheet, Deck Framing and Floor Plans, Deck Elevations, and a Deck Materials List. A Standard Deck Details Package, also available, provides all the how-to information necessary for building any deck. Get both the Deck Plan and the Standard Deck Details Package for one low price in our Complete Deck Building Package.

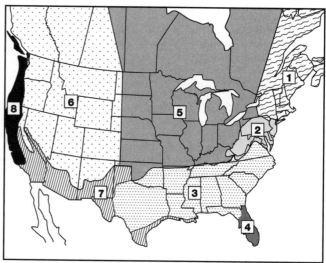

LANDSCAPE BLUEPRINT PACKAGE

Homes marked with an **L** in this book have a front-yard Landscape Plan that is complementary in design to the house plan. These comprehensive Landscape Blueprint Packages include a Frontal Sheet, Plan View, Regionalized Plant & Materials List, a sheet on Planting and Maintaining Your Landscape, Zone Maps, and a Plant Size and Description Guide. Each set of blueprints is a full 18" x 24" with clear, complete instructions in easy-to-read type.

Our Landscape Plans are available with a Plant & Materials List adapted by horticultural experts to eight regions of the country. Please specify from the following regions when ordering your plan:

Region 1: Northeast
Region 2: Mid-Atlantic
Region 3: Deep South
Region 4: Florida & Gulf Coast
Region 5: Midwest
Region 6: Rocky Mountains
Region 7: Southern California & Desert Southwest
Region 8: Northern California & Pacific Northwest

OUR EXCHANGE POLICY

With the exception of reproducible plan orders, we will exchange your entire first order for an equal or greater number of blueprints within our plan collection within **60 days** of the original order. The entire content of your original order must be returned before an exchange will be processed. Please call our customer service department at 1-888-690-1116 for your return authorization number and shipping instructions. If the returned blueprints look used, redlined, or copied, we will not honor your exchange. Fees for exchanging your blueprints are as follows: 20% of the amount of the original order, plus the difference in cost if exchanging for a design in a higher price bracket or less the difference in cost if exchanging for a design in a lower price bracket. (Reproducible blueprints are not exchangeable or refundable.) Please call for current postage and handling prices. Shipping and handling charges are not refundable.

ABOUT REPRODUCIBLES

Reproducibles (often called "vellums") are the most convenient way to order your blueprints. In any building process, you will need multiple copies of your blueprints for your builder, subcontractors, lenders, and the local building department. In addition, you may want or need to make changes to the original design. Such changes should be made only by a licensed architect or engineer. When you purchase reproducibles, you will receive a copyright release letter that allows you to have them altered and copied. You will want to purchase a reproducible plan if you plan to make any changes, whether by using our convenient Customization Program or going to a local architect.

ABOUT REVERSE BLUEPRINTS

Although lettering and dimensions will appear backward, reverses will be a useful aid if you decide to flop the plan. See Price Schedule and Plans Index for pricing.

ARCHITECTURAL AND ENGINEERING SEALS

Some cities and states now require that a licensed architect or engineer review and "seal" a blueprint, or officially approve it, prior to construction. Prior to application for a building permit or the start of actual construction, we strongly advise that you consult your local building official who can tell you if such a review is required.

ABOUT THE DESIGNS

The architects and designers whose work appears in this publication are among America's leading residential designers. Each plan was designed to meet the requirements of a nationally recognized model building code in effect at the time and place the plan was drawn. Because national building codes change from time to time, plans may not fully comply with any such code at the time they are sold to a customer. In addition, building officials may not accept these plans as final construction documents of record as the plans may need to be modified and additional drawings and details added to suit local conditions and requirements. Purchasers should consult a licensed architect or engineer, and their local building official, before starting any construction related to these plans.

LOCAL BUILDING CODES AND ZONING REQUIREMENTS

At the time of creation, these plans are drawn to specifications published by the Building Officials and Code Administrators (BOCA) International, Inc.; the Southern Building Code Congress International, (SBCCI) Inc.; the International Conference of Building Officials (ICBO); or the Council of American Building Officials (CABO). These plans are designed to meet or exceed national building standards. Because of the great differences in geography and climate throughout the United States and Canada, each state, county, and municipality has its own building codes, zone requirements, ordinances, and building regulations. Your plan may need to be modified to comply with local requirements. In addition, you may need to obtain permits or inspections from local governments before and in the course of construction. We authorize the use of the blueprints on the express condition that you consult a local licensed architect or engineer of your choice prior to beginning construction and strictly comply with all local building codes, zoning requirements, and other applicable laws, regulations, ordinances, and requirements. Notice: Plans for homes to be built in Nevada must be redrawn by a Nevada-registered professional. Consult your building official for more information on this subject.

TERMS AND CONDITIONS

These designs are protected under the terms of United States Copyright Law and may not be copied or reproduced in any way, by any means, unless you have purchased reproducibles which clearly indicate your right to copy or reproduce. We authorize the use of your chosen design as an aid in the construction of one single- or multi-family home only. You may not use this design to build a second or multiple dwellings without purchasing another blueprint or blueprints or paying additional design fees.

HOW MANY BLUEPRINTS DO YOU NEED?

Although a four-set building package may satisfy many states, cities, and counties, some plans may require certain changes. For your convenience, we have developed a reproducible plan, which allows you to take advantage of our Customization Program, or to have a local professional modify and make up to 10 copies of your revised plan. As our plans are all copyright protected, with your purchase of the reproducible, we will supply you with a copyright release letter. The number of copies you may need: 1 for owner, 3 for builder, 2 for local building department, and 1-3 sets for your mortgage lender.

DISCLAIMER

The designers we work with have put substantial care and effort into the creation of their blueprints. However, because we cannot provide on-site consultation, supervision, and control over actual construction, and because of the great variance in local building requirements, building practices, and soil, seismic, weather, and other conditions, **WE MAKE NO WARRANTY OF ANY KIND, EXPRESS OR IMPLIED, WITH RESPECT TO THE CONTENT OR USE OF THE BLUEPRINTS, INCLUDING BUT NOT LIMITED TO ANY WARRANTY OF MERCHANTABILITY OR OF FITNESS FOR A PARTICULAR PURPOSE. ITEMS, PRICES, TERMS, AND CONDITIONS ARE SUBJECT TO CHANGE WITHOUT NOTICE.**

IT'S EASY TO ORDER JUST VISIT EPLANS.COM OR CALL TOLL-FREE 1-800-521-6797

OPEN 24 HOURS, 7 DAYS A WEEK
If we receive your order by 3:00 p.m. EST, Monday-Friday, we'll process it and ship within two business days. When ordering by phone, please have your credit card or check information ready.

CANADIAN CUSTOMERS
Order Toll Free 1-877-223-6389

ONLINE ORDERING
Go to: www.eplans.com

After you have received your order, call our customer service experts at 1-888-690-1116 if you have any questions.

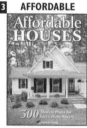

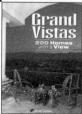

31 NATURAL LIGHT

223 Sunny home plans
for all regions.
240 pgs. $8.95 NA

32 NOSTALGIA

100 Time-Honored
designs updated with
today's features.
224 pgs. $14.95 NOS

33 DREAM HOMES

50 luxury home plans.
Over 300 illustrations.
256 pgs. $19.95 SOD2

34 NARROW-LOT

245 versatile designs
up to 50 feet wide.
256 pgs. $9.95 NL2

35 SMALL HOUSES

Innovative plans for
sensible lifestyles.
224 pgs. $8.95 SM2

36 OUTDOOR

74 easy-to-build designs,
lets you create and build
your own backyard oasis.
128 pgs. $9.95 YG2

37 GARAGES

145 exciting projects from
64 to 1,900 square feet.
160 pgs. $9.95 GG2

38 PLANNER

A Planner for Building or
Remodeling your Home.
318 pgs. $17.95 SCDH

39 HOME BUILDING

Everything you need to know
to work with contractors
and subcontractors.
212 pgs. $14.95 HBP

40 RURAL BUILDING

Everything you need to
know to build your
home in the country.
232 pgs. $14.95 BYC

41 VACATION HOMES

Your complete guide
to building your
vacation home.
224 pgs. $14.95 BYV

42 DECKS

A brand new collection
of 120 beautiful and
practical decks.
144 pgs. $9.95 DP2

43 GARDENS & MORE

225 gardens, landscapes,
decks and more to
enhance every home.
320 pgs. $19.95 GLP

44 EASY-CARE

41 special landscapes
designed for beauty and
low maintenance.
160 pgs. $14.95 ECL

45 BACKYARDS

40 designs focused solely on
creating your own specially
themed backyard oasis.
160 pgs. $14.95 BYL

46 BEDS & BORDERS

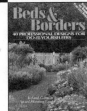

40 Professional designs
for do-it-yourselfers
160 pgs. $14.95 BB

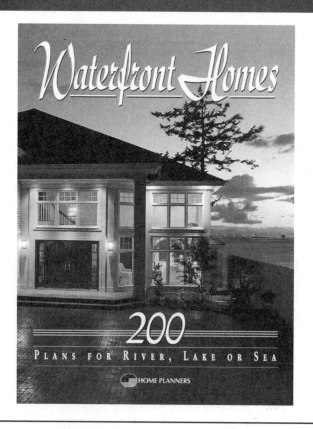

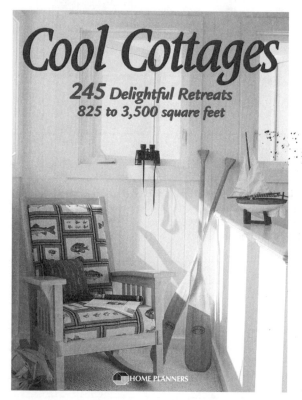